MW01479403

pil
Publications International, Ltd.

Louis Weber, CEO
Publications International, Ltd.
8140 Lehigh Ave
Morton Grove, IL 60053

Pictured on the front cover *(clockwise from top left):* Mushroom Po-Boys *(page 96),* Cauliflower Tacos with Chipotle Crema *(page 102),* Garlic "Bread" *(page 126),* Southwestern Flatbread with Black Beans and Corn *(page 10),* One-Pot Spaghetti Ragù *(page 162),* Beet and Walnut Burgers *(page 82)* and Cornmeal-Crusted Cauliflower Steaks *(page 110).*

Pictured on the back cover *(clockwise from top):* Tofu, Black Bean and Corn Chili Burritos *(page 99),* Chocolate Chip Cookies *(page 169)* and Superfood Kale Salad *(page 58).*

ISBN: 978-1-63938-153-1

Manufactured in China.

8 7 6 5 4 3 2 1

Microwave Cooking: Microwave ovens vary in wattage. Use the cooking times as guidelines and check for doneness before adding more time.

WARNING: Food preparation, baking and cooking involve inherent dangers: misuse of electric products, sharp electric tools, boiling water, hot stoves, allergic reactions, foodborne illnesses and the like, pose numerous potential risks. Publications International, Ltd. (PIL) assumes no responsibility or liability for any damages you may experience as a result of following recipes, instructions, tips or advice in this publication.

While we hope this publication helps you find new ways to eat delicious foods, you may not always achieve the results desired due to variations in ingredients, cooking temperatures, typos, errors, omissions or individual cooking abilities.

Let's get social!

 @Publications_International

 @PublicationsInternational

www.pilbooks.com

CONTENTS

CAULIFLOWER TACOS WITH CHIPOTLE CREMA (PAGE 102)

WHAT IS PLANT-BASED EATING?

Plant-based eating sounds easy. Base your diet on plants, right? Yes, but if you mention plant-based in a room full of people, it will mean something different to everyone.

Opinions vary widely on the definition, and feelings can be heated. People who regularly include meat in their diet may think plant-based is eating more plants along with meat, and perhaps reducing the amount of meat. Those who are already vegetarian may think it means giving up all meat, dairy and eggs completely, while others may say that true plant-based eating means a diet comprised of exclusively organic, local and sustainable plant products, with no dairy, eggs or refined grains, sugar and oils.

So then what is it? The answer is pretty much up to you and how far you want to go. All of the examples above are acceptable, and you may find that you want to transition from eating meat to being vegetarian, and then eliminate all animal products from your diet.

For the purposes of this book, plant-based is defined as always vegetarian and mostly dairy- and egg-free. The important thing, however, is to focus on eating mostly fruit, vegetables and grains and not to get caught up in labels.

If you're just starting out, go easy on yourself and make small, positive changes. Adjust your diet incrementally so that you're not overwhelmed with big changes all at once. You want to strike a balance between eating enough plants and not making yourself crazy. The first step is to eat more plants and begin to think of meat, eggs and dairy products as garnishes instead of center-of-the plate items.

WHAT DO I EAT WITHOUT MEAT?

If you're used to thinking of a meal as a protein, a vegetable and a starch, it can be hard to conceptualize a dinner without these traditional elements filling your plate. You can still have that—it just may not look the same as you're used to. For example, Tofu, Black Bean and Corn Chili Burritos on page 99 contains protein (tofu), vegetables (tomatoes, corn) and starch (beans, rice, corn). It's all mixed up so it may feel like you're only eating one thing but everything is there.

If your usual dinner is cheesy pasta, start with Dairy-Free Mac and Cheez on page 152. The creaminess of cheesy pasta is there thanks to sauce made with nutritional yeast and you've upped your dinner game by adding veggies in the form of a flavorful mix of celery, onion and bell pepper.

If your usual dinner is takeout fried rice or pizza, try Vegetarian Rice Noodles on page 148 or Mediterranean Flatbread on page 24 for similar Asian and Italian flavors but with a plantier, healthier spin.

For breakfast, try something like Chai Spiced Brown Rice & Chia Pudding on page 176. You'll have a hearty breakfast of grains, fruit and protein.

ADD MORE PLANTS TO YOUR DAY

Even on days when you're not up for tons of chopping, you can still easily add vegetables to your day. Roasting is an easy and mostly hands-off way to prepare vegetables for many uses.

First, pick your vegetable(s). Potatoes, sweet potatoes, carrots, cauliflower, broccoli, onions, tomatoes, cabbage, fennel, mushrooms, asparagus, zucchini and winter squash all roast beautifully and deliciously. Next, cut them up into wedges, cubes, sticks or florets, making sure the pieces are approximately the same size.

Then, preheat your oven to 400°F, toss the veggies with olive oil, salt and pepper, and any other seasonings you'd like and spread on a sheet pan. Roast for 20 minutes. Check at this point; some vegetables like carrots may be done. Otherwise, stir the vegetables and add another 10 minutes. Keep checking and stirring until they're as browned and tender as you'd like.

Finally, use them any way you'd like! Here are some ideas to get you started:

- Serve as a side dish or snack with a dip: potatoes with ketchup, sweet potatoes with mustard, carrots with tahini, cauliflower with harissa.
- Use as a topping for flatbread or a filling for sandwiches: onions, garlic, tomatoes, cabbage, fennel, mushrooms, asparagus, butternut squash, zucchini.
- Pick one or two roasted vegetables to add to your favorite pasta or rice dish.
- Chop up cold leftover roasted vegetables and mix with lettuce or mixed greens, chickpeas and your favorite dressing for a veggie-packed salad.

TOFU

Adding more tofu to your diet can help you move away from meat without feeling like there's a huge hole left behind. Cook up a batch using the method below and toss it with barbecue sauce, hot sauce, teriyaki, pesto, zhug or any other sauce you're craving. Stuff it in a sandwich, layer it in a bowl or snack on it throughout the day.

Line a sheet pan with foil or parchment paper and lightly brush with oil. Cut the tofu into cubes or rectangles and spread on the pan. Drizzle with soy sauce or sprinkle with salt and toss to coat. Bake at 400°F for 20 minutes or until crispy, turning once. Or use an air fryer if you have one. Cook the tofu at 375°F for 20 minutes or until the tofu is crispy and browned, stirring occasionally.

EAT CLEAN

If you're eating a plant-based diet, you may want to incorporate some clean eating strategies as well.

- Eat foods in their natural state (or as close as possible).
- Avoid processed foods, refined sugars (white sugar) and refined grains (white flour).
- Plan your meals and go shopping with a list. This way you'll be less tempted by unhealthy foods.
- Go through your pantry and get rid of anything old, stale or processed. You'll start fresh and know what you have.
- Stock up on canned beans, tomatoes, water-packed fruit, brown rice, whole wheat pasta, olive oil and frozen veggies. A quick and healthy plant-based meal will be at the ready, and you'll feel less tempted to make unhealthy choices.

CHAPTER 1
BITE ME! APPS

GUACAMOLE BITES

MAKES 12 SERVINGS (2 BITES PER SERVING)

- **2 tablespoons vegetable oil**
- **1¼ teaspoons salt, divided**
- **½ teaspoon garlic powder**
- **12 (6-inch) corn tortillas**
- **2 small ripe avocados**
- **2 tablespoons finely chopped red onion**
- **1 tablespoon chopped fresh cilantro**
- **2 teaspoons lime juice**
- **1 teaspoon finely chopped jalapeño pepper *or* ¼ teaspoon hot pepper sauce**

1. Preheat oven to 375°F. Whisk oil, ¾ teaspoon salt and garlic powder in small bowl until well blended.
2. Use 3-inch biscuit cutter to cut out two circles from each tortilla to create 24 circles total. Wrap stack of tortilla circles loosely in waxed paper; microwave on HIGH 10 to 15 seconds or just until softened. Brush one side of each tortilla very lightly with oil mixture; press into 24 mini (1¾-inch) muffin cups, oiled side up. (Do not spray muffin cups with nonstick cooking spray.)
3. Bake 8 minutes or until crisp. Remove to wire racks to cool.
4. Meanwhile, prepare guacamole. Cut avocados into halves; remove pits. Scoop pulp into large bowl; mash roughly, leaving avocado slightly chunky. Stir in onion, cilantro, lime juice, remaining ½ teaspoon salt and jalapeño; mix well.
5. Fill each tortilla cup with 2 to 3 teaspoons guacamole.

SOUTHWESTERN FLATBREAD WITH BLACK BEANS AND CORN

MAKES 4 SERVINGS

- 2 oval flatbreads (about 11×7 inches)
- ¼ cup prepared green chile enchilada sauce
- 2 cups (8 ounces) Monterey Jack-style vegan cheese alternative shreds
- 1 can (about 15 ounces) black beans, rinsed and drained
- 1 cup frozen corn, thawed
- ½ cup finely chopped red onion
- 1 teaspoon olive oil
- ½ teaspoon kosher salt
- 1 avocado, diced
- 2 tablespoons fresh chopped cilantro
- Lime wedges (optional)

1. Preheat oven to 425°F. Place wire rack on large baking sheet; place flatbreads on rack.
2. Spread enchilada sauce over flatbreads; sprinkle with cheese alternative. Combine beans, corn, onion, oil and salt in medium bowl; stir to blend. Layer mixture on top of cheese alternative. Bake 12 minutes or until flatbreads are golden and crisp and cheese alternative is melted.
3. Arrange avocado on flatbreads; sprinkle with cilantro. Cut into pieces to serve. Serve with lime wedges, if desired.

VEGGIE SUSHI ROLLS

MAKES 24 PIECES (ABOUT 4 SERVINGS)

- **2 tablespoons unseasoned rice vinegar**
- **1 teaspoon sugar**
- **½ teaspoon salt**
- **2 cups cooked short grain brown rice**
- **4 sheets sushi nori**
- **1 teaspoon toasted sesame seeds**
- **½ English cucumber, cut into ¼-inch thin pieces**
- **½ red bell pepper, cut into ¼-inch thin pieces**
- **½ ripe avocado, cut into ½-inch thin pieces**
- **Pickled ginger and/or wasabi paste (optional)**

1. Combine vinegar, sugar and salt in large bowl. Stir in rice. Cover with damp towel until ready to use.

2. Prepare small bowl with water and splash of vinegar to rinse fingers and prevent rice from sticking while working. Place 1 sheet of nori horizontally on bamboo sushi mat or parchment paper, rough side up. Using wet fingers, spread about ½ cup rice evenly over nori, leaving 1-inch border along bottom edge. Sprinkle rice with ¼ teaspoon sesame seeds. Place one fourth each of cucumber, bell pepper and avocado on top of rice.

3. Pick up edge of mat nearest you. Roll mat forward, wrapping rice around fillings and pressing gently to form log. Press gently to seal. Place roll on cutting board, seam side down. Repeat with remaining nori and fillings.

4. Slice each roll into six pieces using sharp knife.* Cut off ends, if desired. Serve with pickled ginger and/or wasabi, if desired.

**Wipe knife with damp cloth between cuts, if necessary.*

NACHOS

MAKES 8 SERVINGS

- 8 (6-inch) corn tortillas
- 1 cup chopped onion
- 1 tablespoon chili powder
- 2 teaspoons dried oregano
- 1 can (about 15 ounces) pinto beans or black beans, rinsed and drained
- 1¼ cups (5 ounces) Monterey Jack-style vegan cheese alternative shreds
- ¾ cup frozen corn, thawed and drained
- 1 jar (2 ounces) pimientos, drained
- 3 tablespoons sliced black olives
- 2 to 3 tablespoons pickled jalapeño pepper slices, drained

1. Preheat oven to 375°F. Sprinkle 1 tortilla with water to dampen; shake off excess water. Repeat with remaining tortillas. Cut each tortilla into 6 wedges. Arrange wedges in single layer on baking sheet or in two 9-inch pie plates. Bake 4 minutes. Rotate sheet. Bake 2 to 4 minutes or until chips are firm; do not let brown. Remove chips to plate to cool. Set aside.

2. Spray medium saucepan with nonstick cooking spray; heat over medium-high heat. Add onion; cook and stir 5 minutes or until onion is tender. Add chili powder and oregano; cook and stir 1 minute. Remove from heat. Add beans and 2 tablespoons water; mash with fork or potato masher until blended but still chunky. Cover; cook over medium heat 6 to 8 minutes or until bubbly, stirring occasionally. Stir in additional water if beans become dry.

3. Spoon beans over chips. Sprinkle cheese alternative evenly over beans. Combine corn and pimientos in small bowl; spoon over cheese alternative. Bake 8 minutes or until cheese alternative is melted. Sprinkle with olives and jalapeños.

VIETNAMESE VEGETARIAN SPRING ROLLS

MAKES 14 ROLLS

- 12 dried mushrooms (1 ounce)
- 1 large carrot, cut into julienne strips
- 2 teaspoons sugar, divided
- Hoisin Peanut Dipping Sauce (page 17)
- 3 cups plus 2 tablespoons vegetable oil, divided
- 1 medium yellow onion, sliced
- 1 clove garlic, minced
- 1 tablespoon soy sauce
- 1 teaspoon sesame oil
- 1½ cups fresh bean sprouts (4 ounces), rinsed and drained
- 14 (7-inch) egg roll wrappers
- 1 egg, beaten

1. Place mushrooms in bowl; cover with hot water. Let stand 30 minutes.
2. Place carrot strips in small bowl. Add 1 teaspoon sugar and toss until mixed. Let stand 15 minutes, tossing occasionally.
3. Meanwhile, prepare Hoisin Peanut Dipping Sauce; set aside.
4. Drain mushrooms, reserving ½ cup liquid. Squeeze out excess water. Cut stems off mushrooms; discard. Cut caps into thin slices; set aside.
5. Heat wok over medium-high heat 1 minute. Drizzle 2 tablespoons vegetable oil into wok and heat 30 seconds. Add onion; stir-fry 1 minute. Stir in mushrooms, garlic and reserved mushroom liquid. Reduce heat to medium. Cover; cook 3 minutes or until mushrooms are tender. Uncover; add soy sauce, sesame oil and remaining 1 teaspoon sugar. Cook and stir mushroom mixture 3 to 5 minutes more or until all liquid has evaporated. Remove mushroom mixture to medium bowl; set aside to cool slightly.
6. Add carrot strips and bean sprouts to mushroom mixture; toss lightly. Place 1 wrapper on work surface with corner at bottom, keeping remaining wrappers covered with plastic wrap. Drain mushroom mixture; place 3 tablespoons mixture on bottom third of wrapper. Brush edges of wrapper with some beaten egg.
7. To form spring rolls, fold bottom corner of wrapper up over filling. Fold in and overlap the opposite right and left corners to form 3½-inch-wide log. Roll up filling to remaining corner and place spring roll on tray covered with plastic wrap. Repeat with remaining wrappers and filling.

8 Heat remaining 3 cups vegetable oil in wok over high heat until oil registers 375°F on deep-fry thermometer. Fry four rolls 2 to 3 minutes or until golden brown, turning once. Repeat with remaining rolls, reheating oil between batches. Drain on paper towels. Arrange on serving plate with bowl of Hoisin Peanut Dipping Sauce. Garnish as desired.

HOISIN PEANUT DIPPING SAUCE

MAKES ABOUT ½ CUP

- 2 tablespoons creamy peanut butter
- 2 tablespoons water
- 1 tablespoon soy sauce
- ⅓ cup hoisin sauce
- ½ teaspoon sesame oil
- 1 clove garlic, minced
- Dash hot pepper sauce

Combine peanut butter, water and soy sauce in small bowl; stir until smooth. Stir in hoisin sauce, sesame oil, garlic and hot pepper sauce.

TWO TOMATO-KALAMATA CROSTINI

MAKES 20 SERVINGS

- 8 sun-dried tomatoes (not packed in oil)
- 1 baguette (4 ounces), cut into 20 (¼-inch-thick) slices
- 5 ounces grape tomatoes, chopped
- 12 kalamata olives, pitted and finely chopped
- 2 teaspoons cider vinegar
- 1½ teaspoons dried basil
- 1 teaspoon extra virgin olive oil
- ⅛ teaspoon salt
- 1 clove garlic, halved crosswise

1. Preheat oven to 350°F. Place sun-dried tomatoes in medium bowl; cover with boiling water. Let stand 10 minutes. Drain and chop tomatoes.
2. Place bread slices on large baking sheet. Bake 10 minutes or until edges are golden brown. Cool on wire rack.
3. Combine sun-dried tomatoes, grape tomatoes, olives, vinegar, basil, oil and salt in medium bowl; mix well.
4. Rub bread slices with garlic. Top each bread slice with 1 tablespoon tomato mixture.

ONION FRITTERS WITH RAITA

MAKES 10 FRITTERS AND 1¼ CUPS SAUCE

- 8 ounces seedless cucumber (about 8 inches)
- ½ cup vegan sour cream
- 1 clove garlic, minced
- 2 teaspoons chopped fresh mint
- 1 teaspoon salt, divided
- ½ cup chickpea flour
- ½ teaspoon baking powder
- ¼ teaspoon ground cumin
- 1 tablespoon minced fresh cilantro
- ¼ cup water
- 2 yellow or sweet onions (8 ounces each), thinly sliced
- ½ cup vegetable oil

1. For sauce, shred cucumber with large holes of box grater. Combine sour cream, garlic, mint and ½ teaspoon salt in medium bowl. Stir in cucumber. Refrigerate until ready to use.

2. For fritters, whisk chickpea flour, baking powder, remaining ½ teaspoon salt and cumin in large bowl. Stir in cilantro. Whisk in water in thin, steady stream until batter is the consistency of heavy cream. Add additional water by teaspoonfuls if batter is too thick. Stir in onions until coated with batter.

3. Heat oil in large cast iron skillet over medium-high heat (the oil is ready when a drop of batter sizzles). Working in batches, drop level ¼ cupfuls of onion mixture into hot oil. Cook 2 minutes or until bottoms are well browned. Turn and press lightly with spatula. Cook 2 minutes or until well browned on both sides. Drain on paper towels. Serve hot with sauce.

STUFFED PORTOBELLOS

MAKES 4 SERVINGS

- 2 teaspoons olive oil
- ½ cup diced red bell pepper
- ½ cup diced onion
- ¼ teaspoon dried thyme
- Salt and black pepper
- ⅔ cup panko bread crumbs
- ⅔ cup diced fresh tomatoes or drained canned diced tomatoes
- ¼ cup nutritional yeast
- ¼ cup chopped fresh parsley
- 4 portobello mushroom caps

1. Preheat oven to 375°F.
2. Heat oil in medium skillet over medium-high heat. Add bell pepper and onion; cook and stir 5 minutes or until tender and lightly browned. Season with thyme, salt and black pepper.
3. Combine vegetable mixture, panko, tomatoes, nutritional yeast and parsley in medium bowl. Place mushrooms, cap sides down, in shallow baking dish. Mound vegetable mixture on mushrooms. Bake 15 minutes or until mushrooms are tender and filling is golden brown.

MEDITERRANEAN FLATBREAD

MAKES ABOUT 32 PIECES

- 1 package (¼ ounce) active dry yeast
- ½ teaspoon sugar
- ⅔ cup warm water (105° to 115°F)
- 2 to 2¼ cups all-purpose flour
- 4 tablespoons olive oil, divided
- ¾ teaspoon salt, divided
- 1 cup thinly sliced onion
- ½ cup thinly sliced red bell pepper
- ½ cup thinly sliced green bell pepper
- 2 cloves garlic, minced
- ½ teaspoon dried rosemary
- ⅛ teaspoon red pepper flakes (optional)
- ½ cup pitted kalamata olives, coarsely chopped

1. Dissolve yeast and sugar in warm water in large bowl of stand mixer; let stand 5 minutes or until bubbly.
2. Add 2 cups flour, 2 tablespoons oil and ½ teaspoon salt; mix with dough hook at low speed 2 minutes or until soft dough forms, adding additional flour, 1 tablespoon at a time, if necessary to clean side of bowl. Mix at low speed 5 minutes.
3. Shape dough into a ball. Place dough in greased bowl; turn to grease top. Cover; let rise in warm place 1 hour or until doubled in size.
4. Preheat oven to 350°F.
5. Heat 1 tablespoon oil in large skillet over medium-high heat. Add onion and bell peppers; cook and stir 5 minutes or until onion begins to brown. Remove from heat. Season with remaining ¼ teaspoon salt.
6. Roll out dough into 17×12-inch rectangle; place on sheet pan. Combine garlic and remaining 1 tablespoon oil in small bowl; spread evenly over dough. Sprinkle with rosemary and red pepper flakes, if desired. Top with onion mixture; sprinkle with olives.
7. Bake 16 to 18 minutes or until golden brown. Cut flatbread in half lengthwise; cut crosswise into 1-inch-wide strips.

SCALLION PANCAKES

MAKES 32 WEDGES

- 2 cups all-purpose flour, plus additional for work surface
- 1 teaspoon sugar
- ⅔ cup boiling water
- ¼ to ½ cup cold water
- 2 teaspoons dark sesame oil
- ½ cup finely chopped green onion tops
- 1 teaspoon coarse salt
- ½ to ¾ cup vegetable oil

1. Combine 2 cups flour and sugar in large bowl. Stir in boiling water; mix with fork just until water is absorbed and mixture forms large clumps. Gradually stir in enough cold water until dough forms a ball and is no longer sticky.
2. Place dough on lightly floured surface; flatten slightly. Knead dough 5 minutes or until smooth and elastic. Wrap dough with plastic wrap; let stand 1 hour.
3. Unwrap dough and knead briefly on lightly floured surface; divide dough into four pieces. Roll one piece into 6- to 7-inch round, keeping remaining pieces wrapped in plastic wrap to prevent drying out. Brush dough with ½ teaspoon sesame oil; sprinkle evenly with 2 tablespoons green onions and ¼ teaspoon salt. Roll up jelly-roll fashion into tight cylinder.
4. Coil cylinder into a spiral and pinch end under into dough. Repeat with remaining dough pieces, sesame oil, green onions and salt. Cover with plastic wrap and let stand 15 minutes.
5. Roll each coiled piece of dough into 6- to 7-inch round on lightly floured surface with floured rolling pin.
6. Heat ½ cup vegetable oil in wok over medium-high heat to 375°F on deep-fry thermometer. Carefully place one pancake into hot oil. Fry 2 to 3 minutes per side or until golden. While pancake is frying, press center lightly with metal spatula to ensure even cooking. Remove to paper towels to drain. Repeat with remaining pancakes, adding additional oil if necessary and reheating oil between batches.
7. Cut each pancake into eight wedges. Arrange on serving platter. Serve immediately.

BEANS AND SPINACH BRUSCHETTA

MAKES 16 SERVINGS

- 1 can (about 15 ounces) Great Northern or cannellini beans, rinsed and drained
- 4 tablespoons extra virgin olive oil, divided
- 2 cloves garlic, minced
- ½ teaspoon salt, divided
- ½ teaspoon black pepper, divided
- 6 cups spinach, loosely packed, finely chopped
- 1 tablespoon red wine vinegar
- 16 slices whole grain baguette

1. Purée beans in food processor. (If necessary, add 1 to 2 tablespoons water for smoother texture.) Remove to medium bowl.

2. Heat 1 tablespoon oil in medium skillet. Add garlic; cook and stir 1 minute. Remove from heat; add ¼ teaspoon salt and ¼ teaspoon pepper. Stir into beans.

3. Heat 1 tablespoon oil in same skillet over medium heat, coating pan with oil. Add spinach; cook 2 to 3 minutes or until wilted. Stir in vinegar, remaining ¼ teaspoon salt and ¼ teaspoon pepper. Remove from heat.

4. Preheat grill or broiler. Brush baguette slices with remaining 2 tablespoons oil. Grill until bread is golden brown and crisp. Top with bean purée and spinach. Serve immediately.

CHAPTER 2
SEXY SOUPS AND STEWS

HEARTY WHITE BEAN MINESTRONE

MAKES 6 SERVINGS

- 5 cups vegetable broth
- 2 cans (about 15 ounces each) cannellini beans, rinsed and drained
- 1 can (about 14 ounces) diced tomatoes
- 2 medium russet potatoes (about 6 ounces each), peeled and cut into ½-inch cubes
- 1 medium onion, chopped
- 3 medium carrots, chopped
- 3 medium stalks celery, chopped
- 2 cloves garlic, minced
- 6 cups chopped fresh kale

SLOW COOKER DIRECTIONS

1. Combine broth, beans, tomatoes, potatoes, onion, carrots, celery and garlic in slow cooker. Cover; cook on LOW 7 hours.
2. Turn slow cooker to HIGH. Stir in kale. Cover; cook on HIGH 1 to 2 hours or until vegetables are tender.

ASIAN SWEET POTATO AND CORN STEW

MAKES 6 SERVINGS

- 1 tablespoon vegetable oil
- 1 large onion, chopped
- 2 tablespoons peeled and minced fresh ginger
- ½ jalapeño or serrano pepper, seeded and minced
- 2 cloves garlic, minced
- 1 cup drained canned or thawed frozen corn
- 2 teaspoons curry powder
- 1 can (about 14 ounces) coconut milk, well shaken
- 1 teaspoon cornstarch
- 1 can (about 14 ounces) vegetable broth
- 1 tablespoon soy sauce, plus more to taste
- 4 sweet potatoes, peeled and cut into ¾-inch cubes
- Hot cooked jasmine or long grain rice
- Chopped fresh cilantro (optional)

SLOW COOKER DIRECTIONS

1. Heat oil in large skillet over medium heat. Add onion, ginger, jalapeño and garlic; cook 5 minutes or until onion softens, stirring occasionally. Remove from heat. Stir in drained corn and curry powder.

2. Whisk coconut milk and cornstarch together in slow cooker. Stir in broth and 1 tablespoon soy sauce. Carefully add sweet potatoes then top with curried corn. Cover; cook on LOW 5 to 6 hours or until sweet potatoes are tender.

3. Stir gently to smooth cooking liquid (coconut milk may look curdled) without breaking up sweet potatoes. Adjust seasoning to taste with additional soy sauce. Spoon over rice in serving bowls and sprinkle with cilantro, if desired.

CURRY RED LENTIL AND CHICKPEA STEW

MAKES 6 SERVINGS

- 1 tablespoon olive oil
- 1 onion, chopped
- 3 cloves garlic, minced
- 2 tablespoons minced fresh ginger
- 1 tablespoon curry powder
- 2 teaspoons ground turmeric
- 1½ teaspoons salt
- ⅛ teaspoon ground red pepper
- 1 container (32 ounces) vegetable broth
- 1¼ cups uncooked red lentils (8 ounces)
- 1 can (about 15 ounces) chickpeas, rinsed and drained
- 1 can (about 14 ounces) coconut milk
- 1 package (5 ounces) baby spinach

1. Heat oil in large saucepan over medium-high heat. Add onion; cook and stir 5 minutes or until softened. Add garlic, ginger, curry powder, turmeric, salt and red pepper; cook and stir 1 minute. Add broth; bring to a boil. Stir in lentils; cook 15 minutes.

2. Stir in chickpeas and coconut milk; cook 5 to 10 minutes or until lentils are tender, chickpeas are heated through and stew is slightly thickened. Add spinach; cook and stir 2 to 3 minutes or just until spinach is wilted.

FASOLADA (GREEK WHITE BEAN SOUP)

MAKES 4 TO 6 SERVINGS

- 4 tablespoons olive oil, divided
- 1 large onion, diced
- 3 stalks celery, diced
- 3 carrots, diced
- 4 cloves garlic, minced
- ¼ cup tomato paste
- 1 teaspoon salt
- 1 teaspoon dried oregano
- ½ teaspoon ground cumin
- ¼ teaspoon black pepper
- 1 bay leaf
- 1 container (32 ounces) vegetable broth
- 3 cans (15 ounces each) cannellini beans, rinsed and drained
- 2 tablespoons lemon juice
- ¼ cup minced fresh parsley

1. Heat 2 tablespoons oil in large saucepan over medium-high heat. Add onion, celery and carrots; cook and stir 8 to 10 minutes or until vegetables are softened. Stir in garlic; cook and stir 30 seconds. Stir in tomato paste, salt, oregano, cumin, pepper and bay leaf; cook and stir 30 seconds.

2. Stir in broth; bring to a boil. Stir in beans; return to a boil. Reduce heat to medium-low. Simmer 30 minutes. Stir in remaining 2 tablespoons oil and lemon juice. Remove and discard bay leaf. Sprinkle with parsley just before serving.

COCONUT CAULIFLOWER CREAM SOUP

MAKES 6 SERVINGS

- 1 tablespoon coconut or vegetable oil
- 1 medium onion, chopped
- 1 tablespoon minced garlic
- 1 tablespoon minced fresh ginger
- 1 teaspoon salt
- 1 head cauliflower (1½ pounds), cut into florets
- 2 cans (about 14 ounces each) coconut milk, divided
- 1 cup water
- 1 teaspoon garam masala
- ½ teaspoon ground turmeric
- Optional toppings: hot chili oil, red pepper flakes and/or chopped fresh cilantro

1. Heat oil in large saucepan over medium-high heat. Add onion; cook and stir 5 minutes or until softened. Add garlic, ginger and salt; cook and stir 30 seconds.
2. Add cauliflower, 1 can coconut milk, water, garam masala and turmeric. Reduce heat to medium. Cover; simmer 20 minutes or until cauliflower is very tender.
3. Remove from heat. Blend soup with immersion blender until smooth.* Return saucepan to medium heat. Add 1 cup coconut milk; cook and stir until heated through. Add additional coconut milk, if desired, to reach desired consistency. Top as desired.

**Or blend soup in batches in blender or food processor, cooling to room temperature first if your appliance should not be used to blend hot liquids.*

MEXICAN TORTILLA SOUP

MAKES 4 TO 6 SERVINGS

- 6 to 8 (6-inch) corn tortillas, preferably day-old
- 2 large very ripe tomatoes (about 1 pound), peeled, seeded and cut into chunks
- ⅔ cup coarsely chopped white onion
- 1 clove garlic
- Vegetable oil
- 7 cups vegetable broth
- 4 sprigs fresh cilantro
- 3 sprigs fresh mint (optional)
- ½ to 1 teaspoon salt
- 4 or 5 dried pasilla chiles
- 7 to 8 ounces firm or silken tofu, cut into ½-inch cubes
- ¼ cup coarsely chopped fresh cilantro

1. Stack tortillas; cut stack into ½-inch-wide strips. Let tortilla strips stand, uncovered, on wire rack 1 to 2 hours to dry slightly.
2. Combine tomatoes, onion and garlic in blender or food processor; blend until smooth. Heat 3 tablespoons oil in large saucepan over medium heat. Add tomato mixture; cook 10 minutes, stirring frequently. Add broth and cilantro sprigs; bring to a boil over high heat. Reduce heat to low. Simmer, uncovered, 20 minutes. Add mint, if desired, and salt; simmer 10 minutes. Remove and discard cilantro and mint sprigs. Keep soup warm.
3. Heat ½ inch oil in large deep skillet over medium-high heat to 375°F; adjust heat to maintain temperature. Fry half of tortilla strips at a time, in single layer, 1 minute or until crisp, turning occasionally. Remove with slotted spoon; drain on paper towel-lined plate.
4. Fry chiles in same oil about 30 seconds or until puffed and crisp, turning occasionally. *Do not burn chiles.* Drain on paper towel-lined plate. Cool slightly; crumble into coarse pieces.
5. Ladle soup into bowls; serve with chiles, tortilla strips, tofu and chopped cilantro.

VEGGIE SAUSAGE AND BEAN STEW

MAKES 4 TO 6 SERVINGS

- 2 cups fresh bread crumbs
- 2 tablespoons olive oil, divided
- 1 package (about 16 ounces) meatless Italian or kielbasa sausage, cut into 2-inch pieces
- 1 leek, white and light green parts only, cut in half and thinly sliced
- 1 large onion, cut into quarters and cut into ¼-inch slices
- 1 teaspoon salt, divided
- 2 cloves garlic, minced
- ½ teaspoon dried thyme
- ½ teaspoon ground sage
- ¼ teaspoon paprika
- ¼ teaspoon ground allspice
- ¼ teaspoon black pepper
- 1 can (28 ounces) diced tomatoes
- 2 cans (about 15 ounces each) navy or cannellini beans, rinsed and drained
- 2 tablespoons whole grain mustard
- Fresh thyme leaves (optional)

1. Preheat oven to 350°F. Combine bread crumbs and 1 tablespoon oil in medium bowl; mix well.
2. Heat remaining 1 tablespoon oil in large ovenproof skillet over medium-high heat. Add sausage; cook 8 minutes or until browned, stirring occasionally. (Sausage will not be cooked through.) Remove to plate.
3. Add leek, onion and ½ teaspoon salt to skillet; cook 10 minutes or until vegetables are soft and beginning to brown, stirring occasionally. Add garlic; cook and stir 1 minute. Add dried thyme, sage, paprika, allspice and pepper; cook and stir 1 minute. Add tomatoes; cook 5 minutes, stirring occasionally. Stir in beans, mustard and remaining ½ teaspoon salt; bring to a simmer.
4. Return sausage to skillet, pushing down into bean mixture. Sprinkle with bread crumbs.
5. Bake 25 minutes or until bread crumbs are lightly browned and sausage is cooked through. Garnish with fresh thyme.

NOTE

To make bread crumbs, cut 4 ounces stale baguette or country bread into several pieces; place in food processor or blender. Pulse until coarse crumbs form.

MIDDLE EASTERN VEGETABLE STEW

MAKES 6 SERVINGS

- ¼ cup olive oil
- 3 cups (12 ounces) sliced zucchini
- 2 cups (6 ounces) cubed peeled eggplant
- 2 cups sliced quartered peeled sweet potatoes
- 1½ cups cubed peeled butternut squash
- 1 can (28 ounces) crushed tomatoes in purée
- 1 cup drained canned chickpeas
- ½ cup raisins or currants (optional)
- 1½ teaspoons ground cinnamon
- 1 teaspoon grated orange peel
- ¾ teaspoon ground cumin
- ½ teaspoon salt
- ½ teaspoon paprika
- ¼ to ½ teaspoon ground red pepper
- ⅛ teaspoon ground cardamom
- Hot cooked whole wheat couscous or brown rice (optional)

1 Heat oil in Dutch oven or large saucepan over medium heat. Add zucchini, eggplant, sweet potatoes and squash; cook and stir 8 to 10 minutes or until vegetables are slightly softened. Stir in tomatoes, chickpeas, raisins, if desired, cinnamon, orange peel, cumin, salt, paprika, ground red pepper and cardamom; bring to a boil over high heat.

2 Reduce heat to low. Cover; simmer 30 minutes or until vegetables are tender. If sauce becomes too thick, stir in water to thin. Serve over couscous, if desired.

HEARTY MUSHROOM AND BARLEY SOUP >

MAKES 8 TO 10 SERVINGS

- 9 cups vegetable broth
- 1 package (16 ounces) sliced mushrooms
- 1 onion, chopped
- 2 carrots, chopped
- 2 stalks celery, chopped
- ½ cup uncooked pearl barley
- ½ ounce dried porcini mushrooms
- 3 cloves garlic, minced
- 1 teaspoon salt
- ½ teaspoon dried thyme
- ½ teaspoon black pepper

SLOW COOKER DIRECTIONS

Combine broth, sliced mushrooms, onion, carrots, celery, barley, porcini mushrooms, garlic, salt, thyme and pepper in 5-quart slow cooker. Cover; cook on LOW 4 to 6 hours.

PASTA E FAGIOLI

MAKES 8 SERVINGS

- 2 tablespoons olive oil
- 1 cup chopped onion
- 3 cloves garlic, minced
- 2 cans (about 14 ounces each) Italian-style stewed tomatoes, undrained
- 3 cups vegetable broth
- 1 can (about 15 ounces) cannellini beans (white kidney beans), undrained
- ¼ cup chopped fresh Italian parsley
- 1 teaspoon dried basil
- ¼ teaspoon black pepper
- 4 ounces uncooked small shell pasta

1. Heat oil in 4-quart Dutch oven over medium heat. Add onion and garlic; cook and stir 5 minutes or until onion is tender.
2. Add tomatoes, broth, beans with liquid, parsley, basil and pepper to Dutch oven; bring to a boil over high heat, stirring occasionally. Reduce heat to low. Cover and simmer 10 minutes.
3. Add pasta to Dutch oven. Cover; simmer 10 minutes or just until pasta is tender. Serve immediately.

CHICKPEA AND BUTTERNUT SQUASH STEW

MAKES 2 SERVINGS

- 1 teaspoon canola oil
- ¾ cup chopped onion
- ½ to 1 jalapeño pepper, seeded and minced
- 1 (½-inch) piece fresh ginger, peeled and minced
- 1 clove garlic, minced
- 2 teaspoons ground cumin
- ½ teaspoon ground coriander
- 1 cup cubed peeled butternut squash, sweet potato or pumpkin
- 1 cup canned chickpeas, rinsed and drained
- ½ cup water
- 1½ teaspoons soy sauce
- 1 cup coconut milk
- Juice of 1 lime
- ¼ cup chopped fresh cilantro
- Spinach leaves (optional)

1. Heat oil in medium saucepan over medium-low heat. Add onion, jalapeño, ginger and garlic; cook and stir 2 to 3 minutes or until onion is translucent. Add cumin and coriander; cook and stir 1 minute.

2. Add squash, chickpeas, water and soy sauce to saucepan. Bring to a boil. Reduce heat to medium-low. Simmer 15 minutes or until squash is tender. Add coconut milk; cook and stir 2 to 3 minutes or until heated through. Stir in lime juice and cilantro. Garnish with spinach.

VEGETABLE LENTIL SOUP

MAKES 4 SERVINGS

- 1 tablespoon olive oil
- 2 medium carrots, thinly sliced
- ½ cup chopped onion
- 4 cups vegetable broth
- ¾ cup dried lentils, rinsed and sorted
- 1 teaspoon salt
- ½ teaspoon ground cumin
- ⅛ teaspoon ground red pepper
- 1 medium tomato, seeded and diced
- ½ cup chopped roasted red peppers
- 1 tablespoon lemon juice or white wine vinegar
- 2 tablespoons chopped fresh cilantro

1. Heat oil in large saucepan or Dutch oven over medium-high heat. Add carrots and onion; cook and stir 5 minutes or until onion is translucent.
2. Add broth, lentils, salt, cumin and red pepper. Bring to a boil over high heat. Reduce heat to medium-low. Cover; simmer 45 minutes or until lentils are very tender.
3. Remove from heat; stir in tomato, roasted peppers and lemon juice. Cover; let stand 5 minutes before serving. Garnish with cilantro.

CHAPTER 3
HELL OF A SALAD

QUINOA AND CAULIFLOWER TACO SALAD

MAKES 8 SERVINGS

- ¾ cup uncooked quinoa
- 1½ cups water
- 4 cloves garlic, minced, divided
- 1 tablespoon chili powder
- 1¾ teaspoons salt, divided
- 1¼ teaspoons ground cumin, divided
- ½ teaspoon dried oregano
- ¼ cup plus 2 teaspoons olive oil, divided
- 4 cups coarsely chopped cauliflower
- ½ cup raw pepitas (pumpkin seeds)
- Juice of 1 lime
- Salt and black pepper
- 4 to 6 cups shredded iceberg lettuce
- 2 tomatoes, diced
- 2 avocados, diced
- Shredded vegan Cheddar cheese
- Crispy tortilla strips

1. Rinse quinoa in fine-mesh strainer under cold running water. Place in medium saucepan. Add 1½ cups water, 3 cloves garlic, chili powder, 1 teaspoon salt, 1 teaspoon cumin and oregano. Bring to a boil over medium-high heat. Reduce heat to low. Cover; simmer 15 minutes or until quinoa is tender and most water is absorbed.
2. Meanwhile, heat 1 teaspoon oil in large skillet over medium-high heat. Add cauliflower and ½ teaspoon salt; cook and stir 10 minutes or until tender and browned. Add quinoa to cauliflower; cook and stir until well blended.
3. Heat 1 teaspoon oil in small skillet over medium heat. Add pepitas; cook and stir 3 to 5 minutes or until pepitas begin to pop and are lightly browned. Remove from heat. Season with remaining ¼ teaspoon salt.
4. For dressing, whisk remaining ¼ cup olive oil, ¼ teaspoon cumin and lime juice in medium bowl. Season with salt and pepper.
5. Arrange lettuce on large serving platter. Top with quinoa mixture, tomatoes, avocados, cheese, tortilla strips and pepitas. Serve with dressing.

QUINOA TABBOULEH

MAKES 6 TO 8 SERVINGS

- **1 cup uncooked tricolor quinoa *or* ½ cup *each* red and white quinoa**
- **2 cups water**
- **2 teaspoons salt, divided**
- **2 cups chopped fresh tomatoes (red, orange or a combination)**
- **1 cucumber, quartered lengthwise and thinly sliced**
- **¼ cup extra virgin olive oil**
- **3 tablespoons fresh lemon juice**
- **½ teaspoon black pepper**
- **1 red or orange bell pepper, chopped**
- **½ cup minced fresh parsley**

1. Rinse quinoa in fine-mesh strainer under cold running water. Combine 2 cups water, quinoa and 1 teaspoon salt in medium saucepan. Bring to a boil over high heat. Reduce heat to low. Cover; simmer 10 to 15 minutes or until quinoa is tender and water is absorbed. Remove to large bowl; cool to room temperature.
2. Meanwhile, combine tomatoes, cucumber and remaining 1 teaspoon salt in medium bowl. Let stand 20 minutes.
3. Stir cucumber, tomatoes and any accumulated juices into quinoa. Whisk oil, lemon juice and black pepper in small bowl until well blended. Stir into quinoa mixture. Add bell pepper and parsley; mix until well blended. Taste and season with additional salt and pepper, if desired.

NOTE

For a heartier dish, add some chickpeas. Drain 1 can (about 15 ounces) chickpeas and rinse under cold running water. Stir into quinoa with bell pepper.

CHOPPED SALAD WITH CORNBREAD CROUTONS

MAKES 6 TO 8 SERVINGS

- ½ loaf Cornbread (recipe follows), cut into 1-inch cubes
- 1 large sweet potato, peeled and cut into 1-inch pieces
- 5 tablespoons olive oil, divided
- 1½ teaspoons salt, divided
- 3 tablespoons red wine vinegar
- 2 tablespoons white wine vinegar
- 1 tablespoon maple syrup
- 1 clove garlic, minced
- 1 teaspoon dry mustard
- ⅛ teaspoon dried oregano
- Pinch red pepper flakes
- ½ cup vegetable oil
- 1 head iceberg lettuce
- 1 cup halved grape tomatoes
- 2 green onions, thinly sliced
- 1 avocado, diced
- ½ cup coarsely chopped smoked almonds
- ½ cup dried cranberries

1. Preheat oven to 400°F. Prepare Cornbread. Cool in baking pan at least 10 minutes or cool completely; remove to large cutting board. Cut half of Cornbread into 1-inch cubes when cool enough to handle. Return to baking dish. Reduce oven temperature to 350°F. Bake 10 to 12 minutes or until Cornbread is dry and toasted.

2. Spread sweet potato in 13×9-inch baking pan. Drizzle with 1 tablespoon olive oil and sprinkle with ½ teaspoon salt; toss to coat. Bake 30 to 35 minutes or until browned and tender, stirring once or twice. Cool completely.

3. For dressing, whisk vinegars, maple syrup, garlic, mustard, oregano, red pepper flakes and remaining 1 teaspoon salt in medium bowl; whisk in remaining 4 tablespoons olive oil and vegetable oil in thin, steady stream.

4. Remove outer lettuce leaves and core. Chop lettuce into ½-inch pieces and place in large bowl. Add tomatoes, green onions and half of dressing; mix well. Add sweet potato, avocado, almonds and cranberries; mix well. Taste and add additional dressing, if desired. Add croutons; mix gently.

CORNBREAD

MAKES 9 TO 12 SERVINGS

- 3 tablespoons boiling water
- 1 tablespoon ground flaxseed
- 1¼ cups all-purpose flour
- ¾ cup yellow cornmeal
- ⅓ cup sugar
- 2 teaspoons baking powder
- 1 teaspoon salt
- 1¼ cups soymilk or almond milk
- ¼ cup vegetable oil

1. Preheat oven to 400°F. Spray 8-inch square baking dish or pan with nonstick cooking spray. Combine boiling water and flaxseed in small bowl; let stand 5 minutes or until cooled and thickened.

2. Combine flour, cornmeal, sugar, baking powder and salt in large bowl; mix well. Whisk soymilk and oil in medium bowl until well blended. Add to flour mixture with flaxseed mixture; stir just until dry ingredients are moistened. Pour batter into prepared baking dish.

3. Bake 5 minutes or until golden brown and toothpick inserted into center comes out clean.

SUPERFOOD KALE SALAD

MAKES 4 SERVINGS

MAPLE-ROASTED CARROTS

- 8 carrots, trimmed
- 2 tablespoons olive oil
- 2 tablespoons maple syrup
- ½ teaspoon salt
- ⅛ teaspoon black pepper
- Dash ground red pepper

MAPLE-LEMON VINAIGRETTE

- ¼ cup extra virgin olive oil
- 3 tablespoons lemon juice
- 2 tablespoons maple syrup
- ¾ teaspoon grated lemon peel
- ½ teaspoon salt
- ⅛ teaspoon black pepper

SALAD

- 4 cups chopped kale
- 2 cups chopped mixed greens
- 1 cup dried cranberries
- 1 cup toasted slivered almonds
- 1 cup shredded Parmesan cheese
- 12 to 16 ounces grilled chicken breast strips

1. Preheat oven to 400°F. Line baking sheet with parchment paper.
2. Place carrots on prepared baking sheet. Whisk 2 tablespoons oil, 2 tablespoons maple syrup, ½ teaspoon salt, ⅛ teaspoon black pepper and red pepper in small bowl until well blended. Brush some of oil mixture over carrots. Roast 30 minutes or until carrots are tender, brushing with oil mixture and shaking baking sheet every 10 minutes. Cut carrots crosswise into ¼-inch slices when cool enough to handle.
3. While carrots are roasting, prepare vinaigrette. Whisk ¼ cup oil, lemon juice, 2 tablespoons maple syrup, lemon peel, ½ teaspoon salt and ⅛ teaspoon black pepper in small bowl until well blended.
4. Combine kale, greens, cranberries, almonds and cheese in large bowl. Add carrots. Pour vinaigrette over salad; toss to coat. Top with chicken.

HOUSE SALAD

MAKES 4 SERVINGS

- 1 cup croutons, store-bought or homemade (recipe follows)

DRESSING

- ½ cup regular or vegan mayonnaise
- ½ cup white wine vinegar
- ¼ cup grated Parmesan cheese or nutritional yeast
- 1 tablespoon olive oil
- 1 tablespoon lemon juice
- 1 tablespoon corn syrup
- 1 clove garlic, minced
- ¾ teaspoon Italian seasoning
- ½ teaspoon salt
- ½ teaspoon black pepper

SALAD

- 1 package (10 ounces) Italian salad blend
- 2 plum tomatoes, thinly sliced
- ½ cup thinly sliced red or green bell pepper
- ½ cup thinly sliced red onion
- ¼ cup sliced black olives
- Pepperoncini peppers (optional)

1. Prepare croutons, if desired.
2. For dressing, whisk mayonnaise, vinegar, cheese, oil, lemon juice, corn syrup, garlic, Italian seasoning, salt and black pepper in medium bowl until well blended.
3. For salad, place salad blend in large bowl; top with tomatoes, croutons, bell pepper, onion, olives and pepperoncini, if desired. Add dressing; toss to coat.

HOMEMADE CROUTONS

Homemade croutons are incredibly easy to make and much better than store-bought versions. They make a versatile topping for any salad, soup or even a pasta dish and keep well in an airtight container at room temperature, so make extras to have on hand. Bonus—croutons are a great way to use up stale bread. If you have stale bread but aren't ready to make croutons, put it in a freezer bag and freeze it until you're ready. Preheat oven to 350°F. Cut any kind of bread into cubes. Hearty bread like whole wheat, Tuscan or sourdough works best, but sandwich bread works, too. Spread the bread on sheet pan and drizzle with olive oil. Toss with spatula or hands to coat. The bread should be evenly coated; add more oil if needed and toss again. If desired, season with salt and pepper and dried herbs like oregano, thyme or rosemary. Bake 10 to 15 minutes or until golden brown, stirring once or twice. Cool on baking sheet before serving.

CRUNCHY JICAMA, RADISH AND MELON SALAD >

MAKES 8 SERVINGS

- 3 cups thinly cut jicama
- 3 cups watermelon cubes
- 2 cups cantaloupe cubes
- 1 cup sliced radishes
- 3 tablespoons chopped fresh cilantro
- 2 tablespoons olive oil
- 2 tablespoons lime juice
- 1 tablespoon orange juice
- 1 tablespoon cider vinegar
- 1 tablespoon honey
- ½ teaspoon salt

1. Combine jicama, watermelon, cantaloupe and radishes in large bowl; gently mix.
2. Whisk cilantro, oil, lime juice, orange juice, vinegar, honey and salt in small bowl until smooth and well blended. Add to salad; gently toss to coat evenly. Serve immediately.

MEDITERRANEAN BARLEY-BEAN SALAD

MAKES 4 SERVINGS

- ⅔ cup uncooked pearl barley
- 3 cups asparagus pieces
- 2 cans (about 15 ounces each) dark red kidney beans, rinsed and drained
- 2 tablespoons chopped fresh mint
- ¼ cup lemon juice
- ¼ cup Italian salad dressing
- ¼ teaspoon black pepper
- ¼ cup dry-roasted unsalted sunflower seeds

1. Cook barley according to package directions, omitting salt and fat. Add asparagus during last 5 minutes of cooking; drain. Remove to large bowl; refrigerate at least 2 hours.
2. Stir beans and mint into barley mixture. Whisk lemon juice, salad dressing and pepper in small bowl until well blended. Add to barley mixture; toss to coat. Sprinkle with sunflower seeds.

CHICKPEA PASTA SALAD

MAKES 8 SERVINGS

- 4 ounces uncooked spinach rotini or fusilli pasta
- 1 can (about 15 ounces) chickpeas, rinsed and drained
- ½ cup chopped red bell pepper
- ⅓ cup chopped celery
- ⅓ cup finely chopped carrot
- 2 green onions, chopped
- 3 tablespoons balsamic vinegar
- 2 tablespoons mayonnaise
- 2 teaspoons whole grain mustard
- ½ teaspoon black pepper
- ¼ teaspoon Italian seasoning
- Leaf lettuce
- Cherry tomatoes (optional)

1. Cook pasta according to package directions, omitting salt. Rinse under cold water until cool; drain well.
2. Combine pasta, chickpeas, bell pepper, celery, carrot and green onions in medium bowl.
3. Whisk vinegar, mayonnaise, mustard, black pepper and Italian seasoning in small bowl until blended. Pour over salad; toss to coat. Cover; refrigerate up to 8 hours.
4. Arrange lettuce on individual plates. Spoon salad over lettuce. Garnish with cherry tomatoes.

SOUTHWESTERN SALAD >

MAKES 6 SERVINGS

- 1 can (about 15 ounces) black beans, rinsed and drained
- 1½ cups cooked corn
- 1½ cups chopped seeded tomatoes
- ½ cup thinly sliced green onions
- ¼ cup minced fresh cilantro
- ½ cup vegetable oil
- 2 tablespoons red wine vinegar
- Salt and black pepper

1. Combine beans, corn, tomatoes, green onions and cilantro in large bowl.
2. Whisk together oil, vinegar, salt and pepper in small bowl. Pour dressing over salad; stir gently to combine. Serve at room temperature or slightly chilled.

MANDARIN SALAD

MAKES 4 SERVINGS

- ⅓ cup olive oil
- 2 tablespoons cider vinegar
- 2 teaspoons honey
- 2 teaspoons dried tarragon
- ½ teaspoon dry mustard
- Salt and black pepper
- 1 can (11 ounces) mandarin oranges, drained with 1 tablespoon juice reserved
- 4 cups chopped romaine lettuce
- 1 package (3 ounces) ramen noodles, lightly crumbled*
- ½ cup toasted pecans, coarsely chopped
- ¼ cup chopped red onion

**Use any flavor; discard seasoning packet.*

1. Whisk oil, vinegar, honey, tarragon, mustard, salt, pepper and reserved mandarin orange juice in large bowl.
2. Add lettuce, oranges, crumbled noodles, pecans and onion to dressing; toss to combine.

KALE SALAD WITH CHERRIES AND AVOCADOS

MAKES 6 TO 8 SERVINGS

- ¼ cup plus 1 teaspoon olive oil, divided
- 3 tablespoons uncooked quinoa
- ¾ teaspoon salt, divided
- 3 tablespoons balsamic vinegar
- 1 tablespoon red wine vinegar
- 1 tablespoon maple syrup
- 2 teaspoons Dijon mustard
- ¼ teaspoon dried oregano
- ⅛ teaspoon black pepper
- 1 large bunch kale (about 1 pound)
- 1 package (5 ounces) dried cherries
- 2 avocados, diced
- ½ cup smoked almonds, chopped

1. Heat 1 teaspoon oil in small saucepan over medium-high heat. Add quinoa; cook and stir 3 to 5 minutes or until quinoa is golden brown and popped. Season with ¼ teaspoon salt. Remove to plate; cool completely.

2. Combine balsamic vinegar, red wine vinegar, maple syrup, mustard, oregano, pepper and remaining ½ teaspoon salt in medium bowl. Whisk in remaining ¼ cup oil until well blended.

3. Place kale in large bowl. Pour dressing over kale; massage dressing into leaves until well blended and kale is slightly softened. Add popped quinoa; stir until well blended. Add cherries, avocados and almonds; toss until blended.

MIXED GRAIN TABBOULEH

MAKES 4 SERVINGS

- 1 cup uncooked long grain brown rice
- 3 cups vegetable broth, divided
- ½ cup uncooked bulgur wheat
- 1 cup chopped tomatoes
- ½ cup minced green onions with tops
- ¼ cup fresh mint leaves, chopped
- ¼ cup fresh basil, chopped
- ¼ cup fresh oregano, chopped
- 3 tablespoons fresh lemon juice
- 3 tablespoons olive oil
- ½ teaspoon salt
- ½ teaspoon black pepper

1. Combine brown rice and 2 cups broth in medium saucepan. Bring to a boil over medium-high heat. Reduce heat to low. Simmer, covered, 45 minutes or until broth is absorbed and rice is tender.
2. Combine bulgur and remaining 1 cup broth in small saucepan. Bring to a boil over medium-high heat. Reduce heat to low. Simmer, covered, 15 minutes or until broth is absorbed and bulgur is fluffy.
3. Combine tomatoes, green onions, chopped herbs, lemon juice, oil, salt and pepper in large bowl. Stir in rice and bulgur. Cool to room temperature.

TAOS TOSSED SALAD

MAKES 6 SERVINGS

- Baked Tortilla Strips (recipe follows)
- ¼ cup orange juice
- 1 tablespoon white wine vinegar
- 1 teaspoon olive oil
- 4 cloves garlic, minced
- ¼ teaspoon ground cumin
- ¼ teaspoon black pepper
- 3 cups washed and torn romaine leaves
- 1 cup washed and torn Boston lettuce leaves
- 1 cup julienned jicama
- 2 medium oranges, cut into segments
- 1 medium tomato, cut into wedges
- ¼ cup thinly sliced red onion

1. Prepare Baked Tortilla Strips; set aside.
2. For dressing, combine orange juice, vinegar, oil, garlic, cumin and pepper in small jar with tight-fitting lid; shake well. Refrigerate until ready to use.
3. Combine lettuces, jicama, oranges, tomato and onion in large bowl. Shake dressing; pour over salad and toss gently to coat. Sprinkle with Baked Tortilla Strips. Serve immediately.

BAKED TORTILLA STRIPS

MAKES ABOUT 1½ CUPS

- 2 (6-inch) flour tortillas
- Dash paprika

1. Preheat oven to 375°F. Cut tortillas into halves; cut halves into ¼-inch-wide strips. Arrange tortilla strips on cookie sheet. Spray lightly with nonstick cooking spray; toss to coat. Sprinkle with paprika.
2. Bake 10 minutes or until browned, stirring occasionally. Let cool to room temperature.

COUSCOUS AND BLACK BEAN SALAD

MAKES 4 SERVINGS

- 1⅓ cups cooked whole wheat couscous
- 1 can (about 15 ounces) black beans, rinsed and drained
- 1 cup cherry tomatoes
- 2 tablespoons minced fresh chives or green onion (green parts only)
- 1 tablespoon minced fresh cilantro
- 1 small jalapeño pepper, cored, seeded and minced (optional)
- 2 teaspoons white wine vinegar
- 1 teaspoon olive oil
- ¼ teaspoon salt
- ⅛ teaspoon black pepper

1. Combine couscous and beans in large bowl. Cut tomatoes in half lengthwise, reserving 1 tablespoon tomato juice. Add tomatoes to couscous. Stir in chives, cilantro and jalapeño, if desired; mix gently.
2. Whisk vinegar, reserved tomato juice, oil, salt and black pepper in small bowl until well blended. Pour over salad; toss lightly to coat.

CHAPTER 4
SON OF A BURGER

CHICKPEA BURGERS

MAKES 4 SERVINGS

- 3 tablespoons boiling water
- 1 tablespoon ground flaxseed
- 1 can (about 15 ounces) chickpeas, rinsed and drained
- ⅓ cup chopped carrots
- ⅓ cup panko bread crumbs
- ¼ cup chopped fresh parsley
- ¼ cup chopped onion
- 1 teaspoon minced garlic
- 1 teaspoon grated lemon peel
- ½ teaspoon salt
- ½ teaspoon black pepper
- 2 tablespoons vegetable or canola oil
- 4 whole grain hamburger buns
- Tomato slices, lettuce leaves and salsa (optional)

1. Combine boiling water and flaxseed in small bowl. Let stand until cool; refrigerate until ready to use.
2. Place chickpeas, carrots, panko, parsley, onion, garlic, lemon peel, salt and pepper in food processor; process until blended. Add flaxseed mixture; pulse until blended. Shape mixture into four patties.
3. Heat 1 tablespoon oil in large skillet over medium heat. Add patties; cook 4 to 5 minutes or until bottoms are browned. Add remaining 1 tablespoon to skillet; flip patties and cook 4 to 5 minutes or until browned. Serve burgers on buns with tomato, lettuce and salsa, if desired.

MUSHROOM TOFU BURGERS

MAKES 6 SERVINGS

- 7 ounces extra firm tofu, crumbled
- 3 tablespoons boiling water
- 1 tablespoon ground flaxseed
- 3 teaspoons olive oil, divided
- 1 package (8 ounces) cremini mushrooms, coarsely chopped
- ½ medium onion, coarsely chopped
- 1 clove garlic, minced
- 1 cup old-fashioned oats
- ⅓ cup finely chopped walnuts
- ½ teaspoon salt
- ½ teaspoon onion powder
- ¼ teaspoon dried thyme
- 6 multi-grain English muffins or sandwich rolls, split and toasted
- Lettuce, tomato and red onion slices (optional)

1. Crumble tofu and spread on small baking sheet or freezer-safe plate. Freeze 1 hour or until firm. Combine boiling water and flaxseed in small bowl; let stand until completely cool.

2. Heat 1 teaspoon oil in large skillet over medium heat. Add mushrooms, onion and garlic; cook and stir 10 minutes or until mushrooms have released most of their juices. Remove from heat; cool slightly.

3. Combine mushroom mixture, tofu, oats, walnuts, flaxseed mixture, salt, onion powder and thyme in food processor or blender; process until combined. (Some tofu pieces may remain). Shape mixture into six (⅓-cup) patties.

4. Heat 1 teaspoon oil in same skillet over medium-low heat. Working in batches, cook patties 5 minutes per side. Repeat with remaining oil and patties. Serve on English muffins with lettuce, tomato and red onion, if desired.

ROASTED EGGPLANT PANINI

MAKES 4 SANDWICHES

- 1 medium eggplant (about 1¼ pounds)
- 1 cup mozzarella-style vegan cheese alternative shreds
- 1 tablespoon chopped fresh basil
- 1 tablespoon fresh lemon juice
- ⅛ teaspoon salt
- 8 slices (1 ounce each) whole grain Italian bread

1. Preheat oven to 400°F. Line baking sheet with parchment paper; spray with nonstick cooking spray. Slice eggplant in half lengthwise. Place cut sides down on prepared baking sheet. Roast 45 minutes. Let stand 15 minutes or until cool enough to handle.

2. Meanwhile, combine cheese alternative, basil, lemon juice and salt in small bowl; set aside.

3. Cut each eggplant piece in half. Remove pulp; discard skin. Place one fourth of eggplant on each of 4 bread slices, pressing gently into bread. Top evenly with cheese alternative mixture. Top with remaining bread slices. Spray sandwiches with cooking spray.

4. Heat large nonstick grill pan or skillet over medium heat. Cook sandwiches 3 to 4 minutes per side, pressing down with spatula until cheese alternative is melted and bread is toasted. (Cover pan during last minute of cooking to melt cheese, if desired.) Serve immediately.

BEET AND WALNUT BURGERS

MAKES 8 BURGERS

- 6 tablespoons boiling water
- 2 tablespoons ground flaxseed
- 3 tablespoons olive oil, divided
- 1 onion, chopped
- 1 package (8 ounces) sliced mushrooms
- 3 cloves garlic, chopped
- 2 teaspoons salt
- 1 teaspoon dried thyme
- ½ teaspoon smoked paprika
- ½ teaspoon ground cumin
- ¼ teaspoon black pepper
- ½ cup old-fashioned oats
- 1½ cups toasted walnuts
- 1 large beet (about 1 pound), peeled and grated on large holes of box grater
- 1 can (about 14 ounces) cannellini beans, rinsed and drained
- 1 tablespoon soy sauce
- Hamburger buns or rolls
- Optional toppings: pickles, sliced jalapeño peppers or banana peppers, sliced avocado, sliced red onion, sliced tomatoes, regular or vegan mayonnaise, mustard and/or ketchup

1. Combine boiling water and flaxseed in small bowl; mix well. Set aside until completely cool.

2. Heat 1 tablespoon oil in large skillet over medium-high heat. Add onion, mushrooms and garlic; cook and stir 8 minutes or until vegetables are softened and mushrooms are browned. Remove from heat; stir in salt, thyme, paprika, cumin and black pepper. Cool slightly.

3. Place oats in food processor or blender; process until finely ground. Add walnuts; pulse until nuts are coarsely chopped. Transfer oats and walnuts to large bowl. Place mushroom mixture and beet in food processor; pulse until finely chopped. Add beans; pulse just until blended, leaving beans chunky. Add to bowl with nuts. Add flaxseed mixture and soy sauce; mix well. Refrigerate at least 30 minutes.

4. Heat 1 tablespoon oil in large skillet over medium-high heat. Shape mixture by heaping ½ cupfuls into ½-inch patties; place in skillet. Cook 5 minutes per side or until well browned and heated through. Repeat with remaining beet mixture, adding additional oil as needed. Serve on buns with desired toppings.

EGGLESS EGG SALAD SANDWICH

MAKES 5 SANDWICHES

- 1 package (14 to 16 ounces) firm tofu, drained, pressed* and crumbled
- 1 stalk celery, finely diced
- 2 green onions, minced
- 2 tablespoons minced fresh parsley
- 5 tablespoons vegan mayonnaise
- 3 tablespoons sweet pickle relish
- 2 teaspoons fresh lemon juice
- 1 teaspoon prepared mustard
- Salt and black pepper
- 10 slices whole wheat bread, toasted
- 1½ cups alfalfa sprouts
- 10 tomato slices

**Cut tofu in half horizontally and place it between layers of paper towels. Place a weighted cutting board on top; let stand 15 to 30 minutes.*

1 Combine tofu, celery, green onions and parsley in large bowl. Stir mayonnaise, relish, lemon juice and mustard in small bowl until well blended; stir in tofu. Season with salt and pepper to taste.

2 Divide salad evenly among 5 slices of toast. Top with alfalfa sprouts, tomato slices and remaining toast.

BBQ PORTOBELLOS

MAKES 4 SERVINGS

- 1 teaspoon salt
- 1 teaspoon smoked paprika
- 1 teaspoon onion powder
- ½ teaspoon garlic powder
- ½ teaspoon ground cumin
- ½ teaspoon black pepper
- 4 portobello mushroom caps
- 2 tablespoons plus 1 teaspoon olive oil, divided
- ½ medium yellow onion, finely chopped
- ¼ cup ketchup
- 2 tablespoons apple cider vinegar
- 1 tablespoon Dijon mustard
- 1 tablespoon packed brown sugar
- 1 teaspoon soy sauce
- 4 hamburger buns
- Mayonnaise, sliced dill pickles and/or prepared coleslaw

1. Preheat oven to 375°F. Line baking sheet with parchment paper.

2. Combine salt, paprika, onion powder, garlic powder, cumin and pepper in small bowl. Scrape gills from mushrooms and remove any stem. Cut mushrooms into ½-inch slices; place in large bowl. Drizzle with 2 tablespoons oil; toss to coat. Add seasoning mixture; toss until well blended. Arrange slices in single layer on prepared baking sheet.

3. Bake 15 minutes. Turn and bake 5 minutes or until mushrooms are tender and have shrunken slightly.

4. Meanwhile, heat remaining 1 teaspoon oil in small saucepan over medium-high heat. Add onion; cook and stir 5 minutes or until onion is very soft. Add ketchup, vinegar, mustard, brown sugar and soy sauce; mix well. Reduce heat to low. Simmer 5 minutes. Combine mushrooms and sauce in large bowl; mix well. Serve on buns with mayonnaise, pickles and coleslaw.

MEDITERRANEAN VEGETABLE SANDWICHES >

MAKES 2 SERVINGS

- 1 small eggplant, peeled, halved and cut into ¼-inch-thick slices
- Salt
- 1 small zucchini, halved and cut lengthwise into ¼-inch-thick slices
- 1 red bell pepper, sliced
- 3 tablespoons balsamic vinegar
- ½ teaspoon garlic powder
- 2 French bread rolls, cut in half lengthwise

1. Place eggplant in non-aluminum colander; lightly sprinkle with salt. Let stand 30 minutes. Rinse eggplant; pat dry with paper towels.
2. Preheat broiler. Spray rack with nonstick cooking spray. Place vegetables on rack. Broil 4 inches from heat source 8 to 10 minutes or until vegetables are browned, turning once.
3. Whisk vinegar and garlic powder in medium bowl until well blended. Add vegetables; toss to coat evenly. Serve immediately on rolls.

"BACON" AND AVOCADO SANDWICHES

MAKES 4 SERVINGS

- 12 slices vegetarian bacon
- ½ ripe avocado
- 2 tablespoons regular or vegan mayonnaise
- 1 teaspoon fresh lemon juice
- 8 thin slices whole wheat sandwich bread, toasted
- 8 slices tomato
- 1 cup alfalfa sprouts

1. Cook bacon according to package directions.
2. Combine avocado, mayonnaise and lemon juice in small bowl; stir with fork until smooth. Spread about 1 tablespoon avocado mixture on one side of 4 bread slices.
3. Top each with 3 slices bacon, 2 slices tomato, ¼ cup alfalfa sprouts and remaining bread slice.

TIP

Once peeled, the pulp of an avocado begins to discolor almost immediately. Lightly brush the cut surfaces of the fruit with lemon or lime juice to prevent them from darkening.

LENTIL BURGERS

MAKES 4 SERVINGS

- 1 can (about 14 ounces) vegetable broth
- 1 cup dried lentils, rinsed and sorted
- 1¼ teaspoons salt, divided
- 3 tablespoons boiling water
- 1 tablespoon ground flaxseed
- 1 small carrot, grated
- ¼ cup coarsely chopped mushrooms
- ¼ cup plain dry bread crumbs
- 3 tablespoons finely chopped onion
- 2 cloves garlic, minced
- 1 teaspoon dried thyme
- ¼ cup plain vegan sour cream
- ¼ cup chopped seeded cucumber
- ½ teaspoon dried mint
- ¼ teaspoon dried dill weed
- ¼ teaspoon black pepper
- Dash hot pepper sauce (optional)
- Kaiser rolls, split

1. Bring broth to a boil in medium saucepan over high heat. Stir in lentils and 1 teaspoon salt; reduce heat to low. Simmer, covered, 30 minutes or until lentils are tender and liquid is absorbed. Cool to room temperature. Combine boiling water and flaxseed in small bowl; let stand 10 minutes.

2. Place lentils, carrot and mushrooms in food processor or blender; process until finely chopped but not smooth. (Some whole lentils should still be visible.) Stir in bread crumbs, onion, garlic, thyme and flaxseed mixture. Refrigerate, covered, 2 to 3 hours.

3. Shape lentil mixture into four (½-inch-thick) patties. Spray large skillet with nonstick cooking spray; heat over medium heat. Cook patties over medium-low heat 10 minutes or until browned on both sides.

4. Meanwhile for sauce, combine sour cream, cucumber, mint, dill, black pepper, remaining ¼ teaspoon salt and hot pepper sauce, if desired, in small bowl. Serve burgers on rolls with sauce.

GINGER-SOY GRILLED TOFU SANDWICHES

MAKES 4 SERVINGS

- 1 package (14 ounces) extra firm tofu, drained
- 2 tablespoons soy sauce
- 1 tablespoon dark sesame oil
- 1 clove garlic, minced
- 1 teaspoon minced fresh ginger
- ¼ teaspoon red pepper flakes
- 1 large red or yellow bell pepper, stemmed, seeded and cut lengthwise into quarters
- 1½ cups packed mixed salad greens
- 1 baguette (8 ounces), cut crosswise into 4 pieces and split

1. Pat tofu dry with paper towel. Cut tofu crosswise into 4 slices; place in shallow baking dish. Combine soy sauce, oil, garlic, ginger and red pepper flakes in small bowl; mix well. Reserve 1 tablespoon mixture in medium bowl. Spoon remaining soy sauce mixture over tofu; turn to coat. Marinate at room temperature 30 minutes or refrigerate up to 8 hours in advance.

2. Spray grill basket, grill pan or grid with nonstick cooking spray. Prepare grill for direct cooking over medium-high heat.

3. Place bell pepper in grill basket; cook, uncovered, 4 minutes; turn. Add tofu; cook 4 minutes. Turn pepper and tofu; brush tofu with any remaining soy sauce from dish. Cook 3 to 4 minutes or until tofu is browned and pepper is tender.

4. Add salad greens to reserved soy sauce mixture; toss to coat. Serve greens, bell pepper and tofu on baguettes.

CAPRESE PORTOBELLO BURGERS

MAKES 4 SERVINGS

- 1 cup mozzarella-style vegan cheese alternative shreds
- 2 plum tomatoes, chopped
- 2 tablespoons chopped fresh basil
- 1 tablespoon balsamic vinaigrette
- 1 clove garlic, crushed
- ¼ teaspoon salt
- ⅛ teaspoon black pepper
- 4 portobello mushrooms (about ¾ pound), gills and stems removed
- 4 whole wheat sandwich thin rounds, toasted

1. Prepare grill for direct cooking over medium-high heat. Spray grid with nonstick cooking spray.
2. Combine cheese alternative, tomatoes, basil, vinaigrette, garlic, salt and pepper in small bowl.
3. Grill mushroom caps 5 minutes on each side or until done. Spoon one fourth of tomato mixture into each cap. Grill 3 minutes or until cheese alternative is melted. Serve on sandwich thins.

NOTE

Mushrooms can be broiled instead of grilled. Preheat broiler. Line baking sheet with foil; spray with nonstick cooking spray. Place mushrooms, cap side up, on baking sheet. Broil 5 minutes. Turn mushrooms over; fill with tomato mixture and broil 3 minutes.

MUSHROOM PO-BOYS

MAKES 4 SERVINGS

- Rèmoulade Sauce (recipe follows)*
- 1 cup buttermilk
- 1 tablespoon hot pepper sauce
- 1¼ cups all-purpose flour
- 1 teaspoon salt
- 1 teaspoon smoked paprika
- ¼ teaspoon onion powder
- ¼ teaspoon black pepper
- 1 package (4 ounces) sliced shiitake mushrooms
- 1 package (3 ounces) oyster mushrooms, cut into 2-inch or bite-size pieces
- Vegetable oil for frying
- 1 loaf French bread, ends trimmed, cut into 4 pieces and split
- Sliced fresh tomatoes and finely shredded iceberg lettuce

**Or substitute plain mayonnaise for serving.*

1. Prepare Rèmoulade Sauce; cover and refrigerate until ready to use.
2. Combine buttermilk and hot pepper sauce in medium bowl. Whisk flour, salt, paprika, onion powder and black pepper in another medium bowl. Dip mushroom pieces, a few at a time, in buttermilk mixture; roll in flour mixture to coat. Dip again in buttermilk mixture and roll in flour mixture; place on plate. Repeat until all mushrooms are coated.
3. Pour 2 inches of oil into large saucepan; heat over medium-high heat to 360°F. Adjust heat to maintain temperature during cooking. Working in batches, add mushrooms to hot oil; cook 2 to 3 minutes or until mushrooms are golden brown. Remove with slotted spoon; drain on paper towel-lined plate.
4. Serve mushrooms on French bread with tomatoes, lettuce and Rèmoulade sauce.

RÈMOULADE SAUCE

Combine ½ cup mayonnaise; 2 tablespoons Dijon or coarse-grain mustard; 1 tablespoon lemon juice; 1 clove garlic, minced; and ½ teaspoon hot pepper sauce in small bowl.

CHAPTER 5
HARD CORE MAIN DISHES

TOFU, BLACK BEAN AND CORN CHILI BURRITOS

MAKES 8 SERVINGS

- 1 can (about 15 ounces) black beans, rinsed and drained
- 1 can (about 14 ounces) diced tomatoes with green pepper, celery and onion
- 8 ounces firm tofu, crumbled
- 1 cup mild prepared salsa
- 1 cup vegetable broth
- ½ cup frozen corn
- 1 tablespoon chili powder
- 1 teaspoon ground cumin
- 1 teaspoon salt
- ½ teaspoon ground chipotle pepper
- ½ teaspoon dried oregano
- 2 cups cooked rice
- Flour tortillas (8 to 10 inches)
- Optional toppings: sliced avocado, lettuce and/or chopped fresh cilantro

1 Combine beans, tomatoes, tofu, salsa, broth, corn, chili powder, cumin, salt, chipotle pepper and oregano in large saucepan. Cover; cook over medium-low heat 45 minutes to 1 hour or until flavors have blended, stirring occasionally and adding water by tablespoons if mixture seems dry.

2 Stir rice into bean mixture. Top each tortilla with about 1½ cups bean mixture. Fold short ends of each tortilla over part of filling then roll up jelly-roll style. Serve with desired toppings.

MUJADARA

MAKES 4 TO 6 SERVINGS

- 1 cup brown lentils, rinsed and sorted
- ¼ cup plus 1 tablespoon olive oil, divided
- 3 sweet onions, thinly sliced
- 2½ teaspoons salt, divided
- 1½ teaspoons ground cumin
- 1 teaspoon ground allspice
- 1 cinnamon stick
- 1 bay leaf
- ⅛ to ¼ teaspoon ground red pepper
- ¾ cup uncooked long grain rice, rinsed and drained
- 3 cups vegetable broth or water
- 1 cucumber
- 1 cup vegan sour cream
- Pita bread

1. Place lentils in medium saucepan; cover with water by 1 inch. Bring to a boil over medium-high heat. Reduce heat to medium-low. Simmer 10 minutes. Drain and rinse under cold water.

2. Meanwhile, heat ¼ cup oil in large saucepan or Dutch oven. Add onions and 1 teaspoon salt; cook and stir 15 minutes or until golden and parts are crispy. Remove most of onions to small bowl, leaving about ½ cup in saucepan.*

3. Add remaining 1 tablespoon oil to saucepan with onions; heat over medium-high heat. Add cumin, allspice, cinnamon stick, bay leaf and red pepper; cook and stir 30 seconds. Add rice; cook and stir 2 to 3 minutes or until rice is lightly toasted. Add broth, lentils and 1 teaspoon salt; bring to a boil. Reduce heat to low. Cover; cook 15 minutes or until broth is absorbed and rice and lentils are tender. Remove saucepan from heat. Place clean kitchen towel over top of saucepan; replace lid and let stand 5 to 10 minutes.

4. For cucumber sauce, if desired, peel cucumber and trim ends. Grate cucumber on large holes of box grater; squeeze out excess liquid. Place in medium bowl; stir in sour cream and remaining ½ teaspoon salt. Serve lentils and rice with reserved onions, cucumber sauce and pita bread.

**If desired, continue to cook reserved onions in a medium skillet over medium heat until dark golden brown.*

CAULIFLOWER TACOS WITH CHIPOTLE CREMA

MAKES 8 TACOS (4 SERVINGS)

- 1 package (8 ounces) sliced cremini mushrooms
- 4 tablespoons olive oil, divided
- 1¾ teaspoons salt, divided
- 1 head cauliflower
- 1 teaspoon ground cumin
- ½ teaspoon dried oregano
- ¼ teaspoon ground coriander
- ¼ teaspoon ground cinnamon
- ¼ teaspoon black pepper
- ½ cup vegan sour cream
- 2 teaspoons lime juice
- ½ teaspoon chipotle chili powder
- ½ cup vegetarian refried beans
- 8 taco-size flour or corn tortillas
- Sliced red onion or Pickled Red Onions (recipe follows)
- Chopped fresh cilantro (optional)

1. Preheat oven to 400°F. Toss mushrooms with 1 tablespoon oil and ¼ teaspoon salt in large bowl. Spread on small baking sheet.
2. Remove leaves from cauliflower. Remove florets; cut into 1-inch pieces. Place in same large bowl. Add remaining 3 tablespoons oil, 1 teaspoon salt, cumin, oregano, coriander, cinnamon and black pepper; mix well. Spread on large baking sheet in single layer.
3. Roast cauliflower 40 minutes or until browned and tender, stirring occasionally. Roast mushrooms 20 minutes or until dry and browned, stirring occasionally.
4. Combine sour cream, lime juice, chipotle chili powder and remaining ½ teaspoon salt in small bowl.
5. For each taco, spread 1 tablespoon beans over tortilla; spread 1 teaspoon crema over beans. Top with about 3 mushroom slices and ¼ cup cauliflower. Top with onions and cilantro, if desired. Fold in half.

PICKLED RED ONIONS

Thinly slice 1 small red onion; place in large glass jar. Add ¼ cup white wine vinegar or distilled white vinegar, 2 tablespoons water, 1 teaspoon sugar and 1 teaspoon salt. Seal jar; shake well. Refrigerate at least 1 hour or up to 1 week. Makes about ½ cup.

PUMPKIN CURRY

MAKES 4 SERVINGS

- 1 tablespoon vegetable oil
- 1 package (14 ounces) firm tofu, drained, patted dry and cut into 1-inch cubes
- ¼ cup Thai red curry paste
- 2 cloves garlic, minced
- 1 can (15 ounces) pumpkin purée
- 1 can (about 14 ounces) coconut milk
- 1 cup vegetable broth or water
- 1½ teaspoons salt
- 1 teaspoon sriracha sauce
- 4 cups cut-up fresh vegetables (broccoli, cauliflower, red bell pepper and/or sweet potato)
- ½ cup peas
- Hot cooked rice
- ¼ cup shredded fresh basil (optional)

1. Heat oil in wok or large skillet over high heat. Add tofu; stir-fry 5 minutes or until lightly browned. Add curry paste and garlic; cook and stir 1 minute or until tofu is coated.
2. Add pumpkin, coconut milk, broth, salt and sriracha; bring to a boil. Stir in vegetables. Reduce heat to medium. Cover; simmer 20 minutes or until vegetables are tender.
3. Stir in peas; cook 1 minute or until heated through. Serve with rice; top with basil, if desired.

GINGER TOFU BOWL

MAKES 4 SERVINGS

- 7 tablespoons soy sauce, divided
- 2 teaspoons minced fresh ginger
- 1 teaspoon dark sesame oil
- 1 package (about 16 ounces) firm tofu, drained and cut into ½-inch cubes
- 1 cup uncooked brown rice
- ½ seedless cucumber, thinly sliced
- ¼ teaspoon salt
- ¼ teaspoon sugar
- ¼ cup rice vinegar
- 1 teaspoon olive oil
- 1 package (8 ounces) sliced cremini or white mushrooms
- 1 cup thawed frozen shelled edamame
- 2 carrots, julienned or thinly sliced
- 4 green onions, thinly sliced
- Pickled ginger
- Sesame seeds

1. Combine 6 tablespoons soy sauce, ginger and sesame oil in large resealable food storage bag or large shallow bowl. Add tofu; seal bag and turn to coat. Refrigerate 2 hours or overnight.
2. Prepare rice according to package directions.
3. Meanwhile, place cucumbers in shallow bowl. Sprinkle with salt and sugar; toss to coat. Add vinegar; mix well.
4. Heat 1 teaspoon olive oil in medium skillet. Add mushrooms; cook and stir 5 minutes or until mushrooms are tender and lightly browned. Remove from heat; stir in remaining 1 tablespoon soy sauce.
5. Divide rice among four bowls. Arrange tofu, mushrooms, cucumbers, edamame and carrots over rice. Top with green onions, pickled ginger and sesame seeds.

SRIRACHA HOT

CHILI STUFFED POTATOES

MAKES 4 SERVINGS

- 4 medium baking potatoes
- 1 tablespoon vegetable oil
- 1 cup chopped onion
- ½ cup chopped green bell pepper
- 2 cloves garlic, minced
- 1 can (about 15 ounces) kidney beans, rinsed and drained
- 1 can (about 14 ounces) diced tomatoes
- 1 can (4 ounces) diced mild green chiles
- ¼ cup chopped fresh cilantro or parsley
- 2 teaspoons chili powder
- 1 teaspoon ground cumin
- ½ teaspoon salt
- ¼ teaspoon ground red pepper

1. Preheat oven to 350°F. Scrub potatoes; pierce with fork. Bake 1¼ to 1½ hours or until tender.
2. Meanwhile, heat oil in medium saucepan over medium heat. Add onion, bell pepper and garlic; cook and stir 5 minutes or until vegetables are tender. Stir in beans, tomatoes, chiles, cilantro, chili powder, cumin, salt and red pepper. Bring to a boil over high heat. Reduce heat to medium-low. Cover; simmer 8 minutes, stirring occasionally.
3. Gently roll potatoes to loosen pulp. Cut crisscross slit in each potato. Place potatoes on four plates. Press potato ends to open slits. Spoon bean mixture over potatoes.

CORNMEAL-CRUSTED CAULIFLOWER STEAKS

MAKES 4 SERVINGS

- ½ cup cornmeal
- ¼ cup cornstarch
- 1 teaspoon salt
- 1 teaspoon dried sage
- ½ teaspoon garlic powder
- Black pepper
- ½ cup oatmilk
- 2 heads cauliflower
- 4 tablespoons olive oil
- Prepared coleslaw and barbecue sauce (optional)

1. Preheat oven to 400°F. Line baking sheet with parchment paper.
2. Combine cornmeal, cornstarch, salt, sage and garlic powder in shallow bowl or baking pan. Season with pepper. Pour oatmilk into another shallow bowl.
3. Turn cauliflower stem side up on cutting board. Trim away leaves, leaving stem intact. Slice through stem into 3 slices. Trim off excess florets from end slices, creating flat "steaks." Repeat with remaining cauliflower. Reserve extra cauliflower for another use.
4. Dip cauliflower slices into oatmilk to coat both sides. Place in cornmeal mixture; pat onto all sides of cauliflower. Place on prepared baking sheet; drizzle evenly with oil.
5. Bake 40 minutes or until cauliflower is tender. Serve with coleslaw on the side and barbecue sauce for dipping, if desired.

BLACK BEAN AND TEMPEH BURRITOS WITH SAUCE

MAKES 4 SERVINGS

- 2 teaspoons olive oil
- ½ cup chopped onion
- ½ cup chopped green bell pepper
- 2 cloves garlic, minced
- 2 teaspoons chili powder
- 2 cans (about 14 ounces each) stewed tomatoes
- 1 teaspoon dried oregano
- ½ teaspoon dried coriander
- 1 can (about 15 ounces) black beans, rinsed and drained
- 4 ounces tempeh, diced
- ¼ cup minced onion
- ¼ teaspoon black pepper
- ½ teaspoon ground cumin
- 8 (6-inch) flour tortillas

1. For sauce, heat oil in large skillet over medium heat. Add chopped onion, bell pepper and garlic; cook and stir 5 minutes or until onion is tender. Add chili powder; cook 1 minute. Add tomatoes, oregano and coriander; cook 15 minutes, stirring frequently.
2. Preheat oven to 350°F. Spray 13×9-inch baking dish with nonstick cooking spray. Place beans in medium bowl; mash well with fork. Stir in tempeh, minced onion, black pepper and cumin. Stir in ¼ cup sauce.
3. Soften tortillas if necessary.* Spread ⅓ cup bean mixture down center of each tortilla. Roll up tortillas; place in single layer in shallow baking dish. Top with remaining sauce. Bake 15 minutes or until heated through.

**To soften tortillas, wrap stack of tortillas in foil. Heat in preheated 350°F oven 10 minutes or until softened.*

BARBECUE SEITAN SKEWERS >

MAKES 4 SERVINGS

- 1 package (8 ounces) seitan, cubed
- ½ cup barbecue sauce, divided
- 1 red bell pepper, cut into 12 pieces
- 1 green bell pepper, cut into 12 pieces
- 12 cremini mushrooms
- 1 zucchini, cut into 12 pieces

1. Place seitan in medium bowl. Add ¼ cup barbecue sauce; stir to coat. Marinate in refrigerator 30 minutes. Soak four bamboo skewers in water 20 minutes.
2. Oil grid. Prepare grill for direct cooking over medium-high heat. Thread seitan, bell peppers, mushrooms and zucchini onto skewers.
3. Grill skewers, covered, 8 minutes or until seitan is hot and glazed with sauce, brushing with remaining sauce and turning occasionally.

FOUR-PEPPER BLACK BEAN FAJITAS

MAKES 4 SERVINGS

- 1 can (about 15 ounces) black beans, rinsed and drained
- ¼ cup water
- 3 tablespoons olive oil, divided
- 2 tablespoons lime juice
- 1 canned chipotle pepper in adobo sauce
- 1 clove garlic, minced
- ¼ teaspoon salt
- 1 medium red bell pepper, cut into strips
- 1 medium green bell pepper, cut into strips
- 1 medium yellow bell pepper, cut into strips
- 2 medium onions, cut into ¼-inch wedges
- 8 (8-inch) flour tortillas
- ¼ cup chopped fresh cilantro
- Lime wedges (optional)

1. Combine beans, water, 2 tablespoons oil, lime juice, chipotle pepper, garlic and salt in food processor or blender; process until smooth. Place in medium microwavable bowl. Cover with plastic wrap; set aside.
2. Heat remaining 1 tablespoon oil in large skillet over medium-high heat. Add bell peppers and onions; cook and stir 12 minutes or until beginning to brown.
3. Heat bean mixture in microwave on HIGH 2 to 3 minutes or until heated through. Heat tortillas according to package directions.
4. To serve, divide bean mixture among tortillas; top with bell pepper mixture. Sprinkle with cilantro and serve with lime wedges, if desired.

FRIED TOFU WITH ASIAN VEGETABLES

MAKES 6 SERVINGS

- 1 pound firm tofu
- ½ cup soy sauce, divided
- 1 cup all-purpose flour
- ¾ teaspoon salt, divided
- ⅛ teaspoon black pepper
- Vegetable oil for frying
- 2 packages (16 ounces each) frozen mixed Asian vegetables*
- 3 tablespoons water
- 1 teaspoon cornstarch
- 3 tablespoons plum sauce
- 2 tablespoons lemon juice
- 2 teaspoons sugar
- 1 teaspoon minced fresh ginger
- ⅛ to ¼ teaspoon red pepper flakes

**Frozen vegetables do not need to be thawed before cooking.*

1. Drain tofu; cut into ¾-inch cubes. Gently mix tofu and ¼ cup soy sauce in shallow bowl; let stand 5 minutes. Combine flour, ½ teaspoon salt and black pepper on plate. Gently toss tofu cubes, a small amount at a time, with flour mixture to coat.
2. Heat 1½ inches oil in Dutch oven or wok. Test heat by dropping 1 tofu cube into oil; it should brown in 1 minute. Fry tofu cubes in small batches until browned. Remove from oil with slotted spoon and drain on paper towels.
3. Pour off all but 1 tablespoon oil from Dutch oven. Add frozen vegetables and remaining ¼ teaspoon salt. Cook over medium-high heat about 6 minutes, stirring occasionally, or until vegetables are heated through. Increase heat to high to evaporate any remaining liquid. Set aside; cover to keep warm.
4. Stir water into cornstarch in small bowl until well blended. Combine cornstarch mixture, remaining ¼ cup soy sauce, plum sauce, lemon juice, sugar, ginger and red pepper flakes in small saucepan; cook and stir over low heat 1 to 2 minutes or until sauce is slightly thickened; stir to mix well. Spoon vegetables into serving bowl. Top with tofu and sauce; toss gently to mix.

SIZZLING RICE CAKES WITH MUSHROOMS AND BELL PEPPERS

MAKES 4 TO 6 SERVINGS

- ¾ cup short grain rice
- 1¾ cups water, divided
- 1 can (about 14 ounces) vegetable broth
- 1 tablespoon soy sauce
- 2 teaspoons sugar
- 2 teaspoons red wine vinegar
- 2 tablespoons cornstarch
- 3 tablespoons peanut oil, divided
- 1½ teaspoons finely chopped fresh ginger
- 2 cloves garlic, thinly sliced
- 1 red bell pepper, cut into short strips
- 1 green bell pepper, cut into short strips
- 8 ounces button mushrooms, quartered
- 4 ounces fresh shiitake or other exotic mushrooms, sliced
- 1 teaspoon sesame oil
- Vegetable oil for frying

1. Rinse rice under cold running water to remove excess starch. Combine rice and 1½ cups water in medium saucepan. Bring to a boil over medium-high heat. Reduce heat to low. Cover; simmer 15 to 20 minutes or until liquid is absorbed. Let cool.
2. Combine broth, soy sauce, sugar and vinegar in medium bowl. Stir cornstarch into remaining ¼ cup water in small cup until smooth. Set aside.
3. Heat 1 tablespoon peanut oil in wok over medium-high heat. Add ginger and garlic; stir-fry 10 seconds. Add bell pepper strips; stir-fry 2 to 3 minutes or until crisp-tender. Remove and set aside.
4. Add remaining 2 tablespoons peanut oil to wok. Add mushrooms; stir-fry 2 to 3 minutes or until softened. Remove and set aside.
5. Add broth mixture to wok and bring to a boil. Stir cornstarch mixture; add to wok. Cook and stir until sauce boils and thickens slightly. Stir in sesame oil; return vegetables to wok. Remove from heat; cover to keep warm.
6. Shape rice into 12 (2-inch) cakes. (Wet hands to make handling rice easier.)
7. Heat 2 to 3 inches vegetable oil in large skillet over medium-high heat until oil registers 375°F on deep-fry thermometer. Add 4 rice cakes; cook 2 to 3 minutes or until puffed and golden, turning once. Remove with slotted spatula to paper towels. Repeat with remaining rice cakes, reheating oil between batches.
8. Place rice cakes in serving bowl. Stir vegetable mixture; pour over rice cakes.

BROCCOLI AND TOFU STIR-FRY

MAKES 6 SERVINGS

2 cups uncooked rice
1 can (about 14 ounces) vegetable broth, divided
3 tablespoons cornstarch
1 tablespoon soy sauce
½ teaspoon sugar
¼ teaspoon dark sesame oil
1 package (about 16 ounces) extra-firm tofu, well drained*
1 teaspoon peanut oil
1 tablespoon minced fresh ginger
3 cloves garlic, minced
3 cups broccoli florets
2 cups sliced mushrooms
½ cup chopped green onions
1 large red bell pepper, seeded and cut into strips
Prepared Szechuan sauce (optional)

**Cut tofu in half horizontally and place it between layers of paper towels. Place a weighted cutting board on top; let stand 15 to 30 minutes.*

1. Cook rice according to package directions.
2. Whisk ¼ cup broth, cornstarch, soy sauce, sugar and sesame oil in small bowl until smooth and well blended; set aside. Cut tofu into 1-inch cubes; set aside.
3. Heat peanut oil in wok or large nonstick skillet over medium heat. Add ginger and garlic; stir-fry 5 minutes.
4. Increase heat to medium-high. Add remaining broth, broccoli, mushrooms, green onions and bell pepper to wok; stir-fry 5 minutes or until vegetables are crisp-tender. Add tofu; stir-fry 2 minutes.
5. Stir soy sauce mixture; add to wok. Stir-fry until sauce boils and is thickened. Serve over rice with Szechuan sauce, if desired.

TOFU SATAY WITH PEANUT SAUCE

MAKES 4 SERVINGS

SATAY

1 package (14 ounces) firm tofu, drained and pressed*
⅓ cup water
⅓ cup soy sauce
1 tablespoon sesame oil
1 teaspoon minced garlic
1 teaspoon minced fresh ginger
1 package (8 ounces) mushrooms, trimmed
1 red bell pepper, cut into 1-inch pieces

PEANUT SAUCE

1 can (about 14 ounces) unsweetened coconut milk
½ cup creamy peanut butter
2 tablespoons packed brown sugar
1 tablespoon rice vinegar
1 to 2 teaspoons red Thai curry paste

**Cut tofu in half horizontally and place it between layers of paper towels. Place a weighted cutting board on top; let stand 15 to 30 minutes.*

1. Cut tofu into 24 cubes. Combine water, soy sauce, sesame oil, garlic and ginger in small bowl. Place tofu, mushrooms and bell pepper in large resealable food storage bag. Add soy sauce mixture; seal bag and turn gently to coat. Marinate 30 minutes, turning occasionally. Soak eight 8-inch bamboo skewers in water 20 minutes.

2. Preheat oven to 400°F. Spray 13×9-inch glass baking dish with nonstick cooking spray.

3. Drain tofu mixture; discard marinade. Thread skewers, alternating tofu with mushrooms and bell pepper. Place skewers in prepared dish.

4. Bake 25 minutes or until tofu cubes are lightly browned and vegetables are softened.

5. Meanwhile, whisk coconut milk, peanut butter, brown sugar, vinegar and curry paste in small saucepan over medium heat. Bring to a boil, stirring constantly. Immediately reduce heat to low. Cook 20 minutes or until creamy and thick, stirring frequently. Serve satay with sauce.

CHAPTER 6
BIG ASS SIDES

PINEAPPLE-GINGER SLAW WITH QUINOA

MAKES 6 SERVINGS

- ½ cup uncooked tricolored quinoa
- 1 cup water
- ¾ teaspoon salt, divided
- 4 cups shredded red cabbage
- 1 poblano pepper, thinly sliced
- ½ cup chopped red onion
- ½ cup chopped fresh mint
- 1 can (8 ounces) pineapple tidbits, drained
- 3 tablespoons sugar
- 3 tablespoons fresh lime juice
- 2 tablespoons canola oil
- 2 teaspoons grated fresh ginger
- Lime wedges (optional)

1. Rinse quinoa in fine-mesh strainer under cold running water. Bring 1 cup water, quinoa and ¼ teaspoon salt to a boil in small saucepan. Reduce heat to low. Cover; simmer 10 to 15 minutes or until quinoa is tender and water is absorbed. Place quinoa in fine-mesh strainer; rinse under cold running water to cool.
2. Combine cabbage, poblano, onion and mint in large bowl. Stir in quinoa and pineapple.
3. For dressing, whisk sugar, lime juice, oil, ginger and remaining ½ teaspoon salt in small bowl until well blended. Pour over salad; mix well. Serve with lime wedges, if desired.

GARLIC "BREAD"

MAKES 14 STICKS (1 STICK PER SERVING)

- 1 tablespoon olive oil
- 3 tablespoons hot water
- 1 tablespoon flaxseed meal
- 1 medium head cauliflower, finely chopped
- 1 cup (4 ounces) mozzarella-style vegan cheese alternative shreds
- 1 cup Parmesan-style vegan cheese alternative shreds, divided
- ¾ cup almond flour
- 2 cloves garlic, minced
- 1 teaspoon salt
- ½ teaspoon Italian seasoning
- Tomato sauce or pizza sauce for dipping (optional)

1. Preheat oven to 425°F. Grease large sheet pan with oil. Stir water into flaxseed meal in small bowl; let stand 5 minutes.

2. Squeeze excess moisture from cauliflower between layers of paper towels. Combine cauliflower, mozzarella alternative, ½ cup Parmesan alternative, almond flour, garlic, flaxseed mixture, salt and Italian seasoning in large bowl; mix well. Pat into 12×10-inch rectangle and about ¼-inch thickness on prepared sheet pan.

3. Bake on bottom rack of oven 30 minutes or until well browned and edges are crispy. Sprinkle with remaining ½ cup Parmesan alternative. Bake 10 minutes or until cheese alternative is melted. Cool slightly. Cut crosswise into seven strips; cut in half lengthwise to make 14 sticks. Serve with sauce for dipping, if desired.

SPICY PICKLED RELISH >

MAKES 6 CUPS

- 8 serrano or jalapeño peppers, thinly sliced
- 2 banana peppers, sliced
- 3 cups cauliflower florets
- 2 carrots, thinly sliced
- ½ cup salt
- 1½ cups olive oil
- 1½ cups white vinegar
- 3 cloves garlic, thinly sliced
- 1 teaspoon dried oregano

1. Layer peppers, cauliflower and carrots in large jar or large covered bowl or container. Sprinkle with salt; fill with water to cover. Cover and refrigerate overnight.
2. Drain and thoroughly rinse vegetables under cold water. Return vegetables to jar. Pour oil and vinegar over vegetables. Add garlic and oregano; cover and shake or stir until well coated. Marinate in refrigerator at least 8 hours.

ROASTED CARROTS, BEETS AND RED ONIONS

MAKES 4 SERVINGS

- 2 medium beets (about 5 ounces each), peeled, cut into ½-inch wedges, and patted dry with paper towels
- 4 carrots, cut crosswise into 2-inch pieces
- 1 medium red onion, cut into ½-inch wedges
- 2 tablespoons olive oil
- 1 teaspoon salt
- ½ teaspoon dried oregano
- ¼ teaspoon black pepper

1. Preheat oven to 425°F. Line large baking sheet with foil; spray with nonstick cooking spray.
2. Combine beets, carrots and onion in large bowl. Add oil, salt, oregano and pepper; toss gently to coat. Pour vegetables onto baking sheet; arrange in single layers.
3. Bake 15 minutes. Stir vegetables; bake 10 minutes or until vegetables are tender when pierced with a fork.

BUTTERNUT SQUASH OVEN FRIES >

MAKES 4 SERVINGS

- ½ teaspoon garlic powder
- ¼ teaspoon salt
- ¼ teaspoon ground red pepper
- 1 butternut squash (about 2½ pounds), peeled, seeded and cut into 2-inch-thin slices
- 2 teaspoons vegetable oil

1. Preheat oven to 425°F. Combine garlic powder, salt and ground red pepper in small bowl; set aside.
2. Place squash on baking sheet. Drizzle with oil and sprinkle with seasoning mix; gently toss to coat. Arrange in single layer.
3. Bake 20 to 25 minutes or until squash just begins to brown, stirring frequently.
4. Preheat broiler. Broil 3 to 5 minutes or until fries are browned and crisp. Spread on paper towels to cool slightly before serving.

PEPPERY GREEN BEANS

MAKES 8 SERVINGS

- 2 tablespoons olive oil
- 2 teaspoons vegan Worcestershire sauce or soy sauce
- 1 clove garlic, minced
- ½ teaspoon salt
- ½ teaspoon black pepper
- 1 pound whole green beans, ends trimmed
- 1 medium onion, cut into ½-inch wedges
- 1 medium red bell pepper, cut into ½-inch slices

1. Preheat oven to 450°F. Line baking sheet with foil. Combine oil, Worcestershire sauce, garlic, salt and black pepper in small bowl; mix well.
2. Place beans, onion and bell pepper on prepared baking sheet. Pour half of oil mixture over vegetables; toss to coat. Spread vegetables in single layer.
3. Bake 20 to 25 minutes or until vegetables begin to brown, stirring every 5 minutes. Add remaining oil mixture; toss to coat. Season with additional salt and pepper, if desired.

ROASTED CURRIED CAULIFLOWER AND BRUSSELS SPROUTS

MAKES 10 SERVINGS

- 2 pounds cauliflower florets
- 12 ounces Brussels sprouts, cleaned and cut in half lengthwise
- ⅓ cup olive oil
- ½ teaspoon sea salt
- ½ teaspoon black pepper
- 2½ tablespoons curry powder
- ½ cup chopped fresh cilantro

1. Preheat oven to 400°F. Line baking sheet with foil.
2. Combine cauliflower, Brussels sprouts and oil in large bowl; toss to coat. Sprinkle with salt, pepper and curry powder; toss to coat. Spread vegetables in single layer on prepared baking sheet.
3. Roast 20 to 25 minutes or until golden brown, stirring after 15 minutes. Add cilantro; toss until blended.

BULGUR PILAF WITH CARAMELIZED ONIONS & KALE

MAKES 6 SERVINGS

- 1 tablespoon olive oil
- 1 small onion, cut into thin wedges
- 1 clove garlic, minced
- 2 cups chopped kale
- 2 cups vegetable broth
- ¾ cup medium grain bulgur
- ½ teaspoon salt
- ¼ teaspoon black pepper

1. Heat oil in large skillet over medium heat. Add onion; cook 8 minutes, stirring frequently or until softened and lightly browned. Add garlic; cook and stir 1 minute. Add kale; cook and stir about 1 minute or until kale is wilted.
2. Stir in broth, bulgur, salt and pepper; bring to a boil. Reduce heat to low. Cover; simmer 12 minutes or until liquid is absorbed and bulgur is tender.

COLORFUL COLESLAW

MAKES 4 TO 6 SERVINGS

- ¼ head green cabbage, shredded or thinly sliced
- ¼ head red cabbage, shredded or thinly sliced
- 1 small yellow or orange bell pepper, thinly sliced
- 1 small jicama, peeled and julienned
- ¼ cup thinly sliced green onions
- 2 tablespoons chopped fresh cilantro
- ¼ cup vegetable oil
- ¼ cup fresh lime juice
- 1 teaspoon salt
- ⅛ teaspoon black pepper

1. Combine cabbage, bell pepper, jicama, green onions and cilantro in large bowl.
2. Whisk oil, lime juice, salt and black pepper in small bowl until well blended. Pour over vegetables; toss to coat. Cover; refrigerate 2 to 6 hours for flavors to blend.

BARLEY, HAZELNUT AND PEAR STUFFING

MAKES 4 SERVINGS

- 3 to 3¼ cups vegetable broth, divided
- 1 teaspoon salt, divided
- 1 cup uncooked pearl barley
- 2 acorn squash, halved and seeded
- 3 tablespoons olive oil, divided
- ¼ plus ⅛ teaspoon black pepper, divided
- ½ cup water
- 1 small onion, chopped
- 1 stalk celery, chopped
- 1 large ripe pear, unpeeled, cut into ½-inch dice
- ¼ teaspoon dried thyme
- ½ cup chopped toasted hazelnuts

1. Bring 3 cups broth and ¼ teaspoon salt to a boil in large saucepan over high heat. Stir in barley. Reduce heat to low. Simmer 45 minutes or until barley is tender. Remove from heat; set aside.
2. Meanwhile, preheat oven to 350°F. Brush cut sides of squash with 1 tablespoon oil. Season with ½ teaspoon salt and ¼ teaspoon pepper. Place cut sides down on sheet pan; add water to pan. Roast 45 minutes or until squash is tender when pierced with fork. Place squash on serving plates.
3. Heat 1 tablespoon oil in large skillet over medium heat. Add onion and celery; cook and stir 5 minutes. Add remaining 1 tablespoon oil. Stir in pear; cook and stir 5 minutes. Add barley, remaining ¼ teaspoon salt, thyme and ⅛ teaspoon pepper. If mixture is dry, add remaining ¼ cup broth. Stir in hazelnuts. Mound into squash halves.

SERVING SUGGESTION

Spoon stuffing mixture into baked acorn or butternut squash halves. Place stuffed squash in preheated 325°F oven; bake 15 to 20 minutes or until heated through.

TIP

To toast hazelnuts, preheat oven to 325°F. Spread hazelnuts on baking sheet; bake 5 to 7 minutes. Place nuts in a kitchen towel and rub to remove skins. Coarsely chop as needed.

PICANTE PINTOS AND RICE >

MAKES 8 SERVINGS

- 2 cups dried pinto beans, rinsed and sorted
- 2 cups water
- 1 can (about 14 ounces) stewed tomatoes
- 1 cup coarsely chopped onion
- ¾ cup coarsely chopped green bell pepper
- ¼ cup sliced celery
- 4 cloves garlic, minced
- ½ small jalapeño pepper, seeded and chopped
- 2 teaspoons dried oregano
- 2 teaspoons chili powder
- ½ teaspoon ground red pepper
- 2 cups chopped kale
- 3 cups hot cooked brown rice

1. Place beans in large saucepan; add water to cover beans by 2 inches. Bring to a boil over high heat; boil 2 minutes. Remove from heat; let stand, covered, 1 hour. Drain beans; discard water. Return beans to saucepan.
2. Add 2 cups water, tomatoes, onion, bell pepper, celery, garlic, jalapeño, oregano, chili powder and red pepper to saucepan; bring to a boil over high heat. Reduce heat to low. Simmer, covered, 1½ hours or until beans are tender, stirring occasionally.
3. Gently stir kale into bean mixture. Simmer, uncovered, 30 minutes. (Beans will be very tender.) Serve over rice.

COLLARD GREENS

MAKES 10 SERVINGS

- 4 bunches collard greens, stemmed, washed and torn into bite-size pieces
- 2 cups water
- ½ medium red bell pepper, cut into strips
- ⅓ medium green bell pepper, cut into strips
- ¼ cup olive oil
- ¼ teaspoon salt
- ¼ teaspoon black pepper

Place collard greens, water, bell peppers, oil, salt and black pepper in large saucepan; bring to a boil. Reduce heat to low. Simmer, 1 to 1½ hours or until tender.

EDAMAME PEANUT SLAW

MAKES 6 TO 8 SERVINGS

- 4 cups thinly sliced green cabbage (about 1 medium head)
- 3 cups thinly sliced red cabbage (about ½ of a small head)
- 1 red bell pepper, thinly sliced
- 1 cup thawed frozen shelled edamame
- 3 green onions, thinly sliced
- 1 carrot, shredded or julienned
- Juice of 1 lime
- 2 tablespoons unseasoned rice vinegar
- 1 tablespoon dark sesame oil
- 2 teaspoons salt
- 1 teaspoon sugar
- 1 teaspoon minced fresh ginger
- 1 cup roasted peanuts

Combine cabbage, bell pepper, edamame, green onions and carrot in large bowl. Whisk lime juice, vinegar, oil, salt, sugar and ginger in small bowl until salt and sugar are dissolved. Pour dressing over salad; mix well. Stir in peanuts just before serving.

NOTE

This can be made at least 1 day ahead of time and will be good for several days. Store in a covered bowl or container. Adjust the salt, lime juice and vinegar just before serving.

BUCKWHEAT WITH ZUCCHINI AND MUSHROOMS

MAKES 6 SERVINGS

- 1½ to 2 tablespoons olive oil
- 1 cup sliced mushrooms
- 1 medium zucchini, cut into ½-inch pieces
- 1 medium onion, chopped
- 1 clove garlic, minced
- ¾ cup buckwheat
- ¼ teaspoon dried thyme
- ¼ teaspoon salt
- ⅛ teaspoon black pepper
- 1¼ cups vegetable broth
- Lemon wedges (optional)

1. Heat oil in large skillet over medium heat. Add mushrooms, zucchini, onion and garlic; cook and stir 7 to 10 minutes or until vegetables are tender. Add buckwheat, thyme, salt and pepper; cook and stir 2 minutes.
2. Add broth; bring to a boil. Cover; reduce heat to low. Cook 10 to 13 minutes or until liquid is absorbed and buckwheat is tender. Remove from heat; let stand, covered, 5 minutes. Serve with lemon wedges, if desired.

TIP

For a different flavor, add pancetta to this dish. Coarsely chop 4 slices pancetta and cook in medium skillet over medium heat about 5 minutes to render fat. Add 1 tablespoon olive oil, mushrooms, zucchini, onion and garlic. Proceed as directed above.

QUINOA & ROASTED VEGETABLES

MAKES 6 SERVINGS

- 2 medium sweet potatoes, cut into ½-inch-thick slices
- 1 medium eggplant, peeled and cut into ½-inch cubes
- 1 medium tomato, cut into wedges
- 1 large green bell pepper, sliced
- 1 small onion, cut into wedges
- ½ teaspoon salt
- ¼ teaspoon black pepper
- ¼ teaspoon ground red pepper
- 1 cup uncooked quinoa
- 2 cloves garlic, minced
- ½ teaspoon dried thyme
- ¼ teaspoon dried marjoram
- 2 cups vegetable broth

1. Preheat oven to 450°F. Line large jelly-roll pan with foil; spray with nonstick cooking spray.
2. Combine sweet potatoes, eggplant, tomato, bell pepper and onion on prepared pan; spray lightly with cooking spray. Sprinkle with salt, black pepper and ground red pepper; toss to coat. Spread vegetables in single layer. Roast 20 to 30 minutes or until vegetables are browned and tender.
3. Meanwhile, place quinoa in fine-mesh strainer; rinse well under cold running water. Spray medium saucepan with cooking spray; heat over medium heat. Add garlic, thyme and marjoram; cook and stir 1 to 2 minutes. Add quinoa; cook and stir 2 to 3 minutes. Stir in broth; bring to a boil over high heat. Reduce heat to low. Simmer, covered, 15 to 20 minutes or until water is absorbed. (Quinoa will appear somewhat translucent.) Remove quinoa to large bowl; gently stir in roasted vegetables.

CHAPTER 7
IMPASTABLE TO RESIST

PUTTANESCA WITH ANGEL HAIR PASTA

MAKES 4 TO 6 SERVINGS

- 2 tablespoons olive oil
- 3 cloves garlic, minced
- 2 tablespoons tomato paste
- 2 cans (about 14 ounces each) diced tomatoes
- 1 teaspoon dried oregano
- 1 teaspoon dried basil
- Salt and black pepper
- 1 can (14 ounces) tomato sauce
- ½ cup pitted Greek olives, sliced
- 2 tablespoons capers, rinsed and drained
- ½ to 1½ teaspoons red pepper flakes (to taste)
- 1 package (16 ounces) uncooked angel hair or vermicelli pasta

1 Heat 2 tablespoons oil in large skillet over medium-low heat. Add garlic; cook and stir until lightly browned. Add tomato paste and cook 2 minutes.

2 Stir in tomatoes, oregano, basil, salt and black pepper. Increase heat to medium. Cook 30 minutes or until tomatoes break down and mixture becomes saucy, stirring occasionally. Turn heat to medium-low. Add tomato sauce, olives, capers and red pepper flakes; simmer 10 minutes.

3 Meanwhile, bring large saucepan of salted water to a boil. Add pasta; cook according to package directions until al dente. Drain and add to skillet with sauce; toss gently to coat.

VEGETARIAN RICE NOODLES

MAKES 4 SERVINGS

- ½ cup soy sauce
- ⅓ cup sugar
- ¼ cup lime juice
- 2 fresh red Thai chiles *or* 1 large jalapeño pepper, finely chopped
- 8 ounces thin rice noodles (rice vermicelli)
- ¼ cup vegetable oil
- 8 ounces firm tofu, drained and cut into triangles
- 1 jicama (8 ounces), peeled and chopped *or* 1 can (8 ounces) sliced water chestnuts, drained
- 2 medium sweet potatoes (1 pound), peeled and cut into ¼-inch-thick slices
- 2 large leeks, cut into ¼-inch-thick slices
- ¼ cup chopped unsalted dry-roasted peanuts
- 2 tablespoons chopped fresh mint
- 2 tablespoons chopped fresh cilantro

1. Combine soy sauce, sugar, lime juice and chiles in small bowl until well blended; set aside.
2. Place rice noodles in medium bowl. Cover with hot water; let stand 15 minutes or until soft. Drain well; cut into 3-inch lengths.
3. Meanwhile, heat oil in large skillet over medium-high heat. Add tofu; stir-fry 4 minutes per side or until golden brown. Remove with slotted spatula to paper towel-lined baking sheet.
4. Add jicama to skillet; stir-fry 5 minutes or until lightly browned. Remove to baking sheet. Stir-fry sweet potatoes in batches until tender and browned. Remove to baking sheet. Add leeks to skillet; stir-fry 1 minute. Remove to baking sheet.
5. Stir soy sauce mixture; add to skillet. Cook until sugar dissolves. Add noodles; toss to coat. Gently stir in tofu, vegetables, peanuts, mint and cilantro.

ROASTED FENNEL AND SPAGHETTI

MAKES 2 TO 4 SERVINGS

- 2 bulbs fennel, trimmed, cored and sliced ¼-inch thick
- 2 carrots, peeled and quartered
- 1 tablespoon plus 2 teaspoons olive oil, divided
- Salt and black pepper
- 1 cup fresh bread crumbs
- 2 cloves garlic, minced
- 8 ounces uncooked vermicelli or spaghetti
- 2 tablespoons fresh lemon juice
- 2 tablespoons chopped fresh oregano

1. Preheat oven to 400°F. Place fennel and carrots on sheet pan. Drizzle with 1 teaspoon oil and sprinkle lightly with salt and pepper (about ¼ teaspoon each). Toss to coat; spread in single layer.
2. Bake 30 minutes or until vegetables are tender and well browned, stirring once or twice. When carrots are cool enough to handle, cut diagonally into 1-inch pieces.
3. Meanwhile, heat 1 tablespoon oil in medium skillet over medium heat. Add bread crumbs and garlic; cook and stir 3 minutes or until bread is toasted. Remove to small bowl; season with salt.
4. Cook pasta according to package directions in large saucepan of salted water until al dente. Drain and return to saucepan. Stir in lemon juice and remaining 1 teaspoon oil. Divide pasta among serving bowls. Top with vegetables, bread crumbs and oregano.

DAIRY-FREE MAC AND CHEEZ

MAKES 4 TO 6 SERVINGS

- 1½ cups uncooked elbow macaroni
- 1 cup chopped onion
- 1 cup chopped red or green bell pepper
- ¾ cup chopped celery
- ¾ cup nutritional yeast
- ¼ cup all-purpose flour
- 1½ teaspoons salt
- ¼ teaspoon garlic powder
- ¼ teaspoon onion powder
- 2 cups unsweetened soymilk or other dairy-free milk
- 1 teaspoon prepared yellow mustard
- 3 drops hot pepper sauce (optional)
- ½ teaspoon paprika

1. Preheat oven to 350°F. Spray 12×8-inch baking dish with nonstick cooking spray. Prepare macaroni according to package directions. Add onion, bell pepper and celery during last 5 minutes of cooking. Drain; return to saucepan.
2. Meanwhile, combine nutritional yeast, flour, salt, garlic powder and onion powder in medium saucepan. Whisk in soymilk over medium heat until smooth. Add mustard and hot pepper sauce, if desired. Continue whisking 10 minutes or until mixture thickens to desired consistency. Pour over macaroni and vegetables; mix well.
3. Spread mixture in prepared baking dish; sprinkle with paprika. Bake 15 to 20 minutes or until heated through.

VEGAN SPINACH-ARTICHOKE LASAGNA

MAKES 8 SERVINGS

- 1 tablespoon olive oil
- 1 cup chopped onion
- 3 cloves garlic, chopped
- ¼ cup tomato paste
- ¼ cup dry white wine
- 1 can (28 ounces) crushed tomatoes
- 1 teaspoon salt
- 1 teaspoon sugar
- 1 teaspoon dried oregano
- Not Ricotta (recipe follows)
- 1 can (14 ounces) artichoke hearts, drained and chopped
- 1 package (10 ounces) frozen chopped spinach, thawed and squeezed dry
- 9 no-boil lasagna noodles
- 2 cups vegan cheese alternative shreds
- 2 roasted bell peppers, chopped

1 For sauce, heat oil in large saucepan over medium-high heat. Add onion; cook and stir 5 minutes or until onion is tender. Add garlic; cook and stir 30 seconds. Stir in tomato paste; cook and stir 1 minute. Stir in wine; cook 30 seconds. Stir in tomatoes, salt, sugar and oregano. Reduce heat to low. Partially cover and simmer 30 minutes.

2 Meanwhile, prepare Not Ricotta. Combine artichokes and spinach in small bowl.

3 Preheat oven to 350°F. Spray 13×9-inch baking dish with nonstick cooking spray. Spread ½ cup sauce in dish; arrange three noodles over sauce. Spread half of Not Ricotta over noodles; top with artichoke mixture, half of cheese alternative and ½ cup sauce. Repeat layers of noodles and Not Ricotta; top with roasted peppers, remaining 3 noodles, sauce and cheese alternative.

4 Cover with greased foil; bake 45 minutes. Remove foil; bake 15 minutes. Let stand 10 minutes before serving.

NOT RICOTTA

Drain 1 package (14 ounces) firm tofu and pat dry. Crumble into large bowl. Add 1 cup silken tofu, ½ cup chopped fresh parsley, 2 teaspoons salt, 2 teaspoons lemon juice, 1 teaspoon sugar and 1 teaspoon black pepper; mix well. Refrigerate until needed. Drain liquid before using.

SOBA STIR-FRY

MAKES 4 SERVINGS

- 8 ounces uncooked soba (buckwheat) noodles
- 1 tablespoon olive oil
- 2 cups sliced shiitake mushrooms
- 1 medium red bell pepper, cut into thin strips
- 2 whole dried red chiles *or* ¼ teaspoon red pepper flakes
- 1 clove garlic, minced
- 2 cups shredded napa cabbage
- ½ cup vegetable broth
- 2 tablespoons tamari or soy sauce
- 1 tablespoon rice wine or dry sherry
- 2 teaspoons cornstarch
- 1 package (14 ounces) firm tofu, drained and cut into 1-inch cubes
- Salt and black pepper
- 2 green onions, thinly sliced

1. Bring large saucepan of salted water to a boil. Add noodles; return to a boil. Reduce heat to low. Cook 3 minutes or until tender. Drain and rinse under cold water to cool.
2. Heat oil in large nonstick skillet or wok over medium-high heat. Add mushrooms, bell pepper, dried chiles and garlic; cook and stir 3 minutes or until mushrooms are tender. Add cabbage; cover and cook 2 minutes or until cabbage is wilted.
3. Whisk broth, tamari and rice wine into cornstarch in small bowl until smooth. Stir sauce into vegetable mixture. Cook 2 minutes or until sauce is thickened.
4. Stir tofu and noodles into vegetable mixture; toss gently until heated through. Season with salt and black pepper. Sprinkle with green onions. Serve immediately.

SPAGHETTI MEDITERRANEAN

MAKES 4 SERVINGS

- 1½ pounds fresh tomatoes (about 4 large)
- 12 ounces uncooked spaghetti
- ¼ cup olive oil
- 2 cloves garlic, minced
- ½ cup chopped fresh parsley
- 1 tablespoon drained capers
- 1 tablespoon chopped fresh basil *or* ½ teaspoon dried basil
- ½ teaspoon dried oregano
- ½ teaspoon salt
- ¼ teaspoon red pepper flakes
- 12 pitted green olives, sliced

1. Bring large saucepan of water to a boil. Add tomatoes; cook 1 minute to loosen skins. Immediately drain tomatoes and rinse under cold running water. Peel, seed and coarsely chop tomatoes.
2. Cook spaghetti in large pot of boiling salted water just until al dente, 8 to 12 minutes; drain. Set aside and keep warm.
3. Meanwhile, heat oil in medium skillet over medium-high heat. Add garlic; cook 45 seconds or just until garlic begins to color. Add tomatoes, parsley, capers, basil, oregano, salt, red pepper flakes and olives to skillet; cook and stir 10 minutes over medium-high heat until most of the liquid has evaporated and sauce is slightly thickened. Pour sauce over spaghetti; toss lightly. Serve immediately.

PENNE WITH SPRING VEGETABLES

MAKES 4 SERVINGS

- ¼ cup olive oil
- ½ cup chopped onion
- 2 cloves garlic, minced
- 1 pound asparagus, cut into 1-inch pieces
- 2½ cups halved cherry tomatoes (12 ounces)
- 2 cups diced yellow squash
- ¾ cup vegetable broth
- ¼ teaspoon salt
- ¼ teaspoon black pepper
- 6 cups cooked whole wheat or multigrain penne
- 1½ cups jarred marinara sauce
- 6 fresh basil leaves, cut into thin strips

1. Heat oil in large saucepan over medium heat. Add onion and garlic; cook 3 minutes, stirring constantly. Add asparagus; cook and stir 4 minutes. Add tomatoes and squash; cook and stir 3 minutes or until tomatoes are softened. Add broth; reduce heat to medium-low. Simmer 6 minutes or until asparagus is tender. Season with salt and pepper.
2. Add penne, sauce and basil to tomato mixture; toss to combine.

ONE-POT SPAGHETTI RAGÙ

MAKES 6 TO 8 SERVINGS

- 1 tablespoon olive oil
- 1 cup chopped onion
- 2 cloves garlic, minced
- 1 package (16 ounces) refrigerated plant-based ground meatless product *or* 1 package (10 ounces) frozen meatless crumbles
- 1 cup chopped yellow, red and/or green bell peppers
- 1 can (about 14 ounces) crushed tomatoes
- 1 can (about 14 ounces) diced tomatoes
- 2½ teaspoons salt
- 2 teaspoons dried basil
- 1 teaspoon dried oregano
- ¼ teaspoon black pepper
- 1 package (16 ounces) uncooked spaghetti, broken in half
- 2½ to 3 cups water, divided
- Grated Parmesan-style vegan alternative (optional)

1. Heat oil in large saucepan or Dutch oven over medium-high heat. Add onion and garlic; cook and stir 3 minutes or until onion is softened. Add meatless product; cook until browned, stirring to break up. Drain fat. Add bell peppers; cook and stir 2 minutes. Add crushed tomatoes, diced tomatoes, salt, basil, oregano and black pepper; mix well.

2. Add pasta to saucepan; stir gently to allow some liquid to get between strands of spaghetti to prevent sticking. Add 2½ cups water. Bring to a boil. Reduce heat to medium. Cover; cook 15 minutes, stirring occasionally. Remove cover and add additional water if pasta seems dry. Test pasta for doneness; continue to cook 2 to 3 minutes or until pasta is desired doneness, stirring frequently. Season with additional salt and pepper. Serve immediately with cheese alternative, if desired.

PASTA WITH AVOCADO AND BELL PEPPER

MAKES 6 SERVINGS

- 1 ripe avocado, diced
- 1 medium red or green bell pepper, diced
- ½ cup oil-packed sun-dried tomatoes, drained and chopped
- ½ cup chopped fresh basil
- 2 green onions, chopped
- 2 tablespoons olive oil
- 6 cups hot cooked multigrain or whole wheat penne or rotini pasta
- ¼ teaspoon salt
- ¼ teaspoon black pepper

Combine avocado, bell pepper, tomatoes, basil, green onions and oil in large bowl; mix gently. Add hot pasta; toss until blended. Season with salt and black pepper.

ASIAN NOODLE SKILLET

MAKES 4 SERVINGS

- 4 ounces soba (buckwheat) noodles
- 2 tablespoons vegetable oil, divided
- 1 package (16 ounces) firm tofu, cut into 1-inch cubes
- 4 cloves garlic, minced
- 1 tablespoon minced fresh ginger
- 1 can (8 ounces) water chestnuts
- 1 cup baby corn
- 1½ cups mushroom or vegetable broth
- 2 tablespoons soy sauce
- 1 cup snow peas
- ¼ cup green onions, thinly sliced

1. Bring about 6 cups water to boil in large saucepan. Add noodles. Boil 1 minute or until tender. Rinse under cold water and drain.

2. Heat 1 tablespoon oil in large skillet over medium-high heat. Add tofu; cook until browned on all sides. Remove to plate. Add remaining 1 tablespoon oil to skillet. Add garlic and ginger. Cook and stir 1 minute or until fragrant. Stir in water chestnuts and corn.

3. Return browned tofu to skillet. Add broth, soy sauce, snow peas and drained noodles; bring to a boil. Reduce heat to low. Simmer 3 minutes or until noodles are cooked through and most of liquid has evaporated. Stir in green onions.

CHAPTER 8
DAMN DELICIOUS DESSERTS

CHOCOLATE CHIP COOKIES

MAKES ABOUT 18 COOKIES

- 2 cups all-purpose flour
- 1 teaspoon baking soda
- ½ teaspoon salt
- ¼ teaspoon baking powder
- ¾ cup coconut oil, melted and cooled slightly
- ¾ cup packed brown sugar
- ½ cup granulated sugar
- ½ cup water
- 1¼ teaspoons vanilla
- 1 package (12 ounces) vegan semisweet chocolate chips
- Flaky sea salt (optional)

1. Whisk flour, baking soda, ½ teaspoon salt and ¼ teaspoon baking powder in medium bowl.
2. Whisk coconut oil, sugars, water and vanilla in large bowl until well blended. Add flour mixture; stir until well blended. Add chocolate chips; mix well. Cover and refrigerate at least 1 hour or until firm.
3. Preheat oven to 350°F. Line cookie sheets with parchment paper. For each cookie, shape 2 tablespoons of dough into 1½-inch ball; place 9 balls on each prepared cookie sheet. Sprinkle with sea salt, if desired.
4. Bake 12 minutes or until centers are set and edges are lightly browned. Cool cookies on baking sheets 5 minutes. Remove to wire racks; cool completely.

NOTE

These cookies are great the day they're made but the flavor and texture are even better the next day.

VEGAN CHOCOLATE CAKE

MAKES 12 TO 16 SERVINGS

CAKE

- 6 tablespoons boiling water
- 2 tablespoons ground flaxseed
- 2 cups granulated sugar
- 2 cups all-purpose flour
- 1 cup unsweetened cocoa powder
- 1 tablespoon instant espresso powder*
- 1½ teaspoons baking soda
- 1½ teaspoons baking powder
- 1½ teaspoons salt
- ¾ cup plain unsweetened almond milk
- ½ cup vegetable oil
- 1 tablespoon apple cider vinegar
- 2 teaspoons vanilla
- 1 cup hot water*

FROSTING

- 1 package (12 ounces) vegan chocolate chips
- ¼ teaspoon salt
- 1 can (about 14 ounces) full-fat coconut milk
- 2 cups powdered sugar
- Colored decors (optional)

**Or substitute 1 cup hot strong coffee for the espresso powder and hot water.*

1. Preheat oven to 350°F. Line 13×9-inch baking pan with parchment paper or spray with nonstick cooking spray. Combine boiling water and flaxseed in small bowl; cool completely.

2. Whisk granulated sugar, flour, cocoa, espresso powder, baking soda, baking powder and 1½ teaspoons salt in large bowl. Make well in center. Pour almond milk, oil, vinegar, vanilla and flaxseed mixture into well; whisk gently to blend wet ingredients. Whisk into dry ingredients until moistened. Add hot water; whisk until well blended. Pour into prepared pan.

3. Bake 35 minutes or until top appears dry and toothpick inserted into center comes out clean. Cool completely in pan on wire rack.

4. For frosting, place chocolate chips and ¼ teaspoon salt in bowl of electric stand mixer. Bring coconut milk to a simmer in small saucepan over medium heat, whisking frequently to blend. Pour 1 cup coconut milk over chips; swirl to coat. Let stand 5 minutes; whisk until smooth. Cool to room temperature.** Add powdered sugar; beat at low speed until blended. Increase speed to medium-high; beat 1 to 2 minutes or until frosting is fluffy and smooth. If frosting is too thick, add remaining coconut milk by teaspoonfuls until desired consistency is reached. Spread frosting over cake; sprinkle with decors, if desired.

***To frost cake with ganache instead of frosting, spread cooled mixture over top of cake (skip the powdered sugar). For firm ganache, refrigerate until set.*

NOTE

This cake keeps very well at room temperature (frosted or unfrosted) for a few days—just cover it tightly with plastic wrap. To make the neatest slices, run a long sharp knife (not serrated) under hot water to warm it and wipe dry immediately. After every cut, rewarm it under hot water and wipe dry as needed.

PLUM RHUBARB CRUMBLE

MAKES 6 TO 8 SERVINGS

- 1½ pounds plums, each pitted and cut into 8 wedges (4 cups)
- 1½ pounds rhubarb, cut into ½-inch pieces (5 cups)
- 1 cup granulated sugar
- 1 teaspoon finely grated fresh ginger
- ¼ teaspoon ground nutmeg
- 3 tablespoons cornstarch
- ¾ cup old-fashioned oats
- ½ cup all-purpose flour
- ½ cup packed brown sugar
- ½ cup toasted sliced almonds
- ¼ teaspoon salt
- ½ cup coconut oil

1. Combine plums, rhubarb, granulated sugar, ginger and nutmeg in large bowl; toss to coat. Cover; let stand at room temperature 2 hours.
2. Preheat oven to 375°F. Spray 9-inch round or square baking dish with nonstick cooking spray. Line baking sheet with foil.
3. Pour juices from fruit mixture into small saucepan; bring to a boil over medium-high heat. Cook 12 minutes or until reduced to syrupy consistency, stirring occasionally. Stir in cornstarch until well blended. Stir mixture into bowl with fruit; pour into prepared baking dish.
4. Combine oats, flour, brown sugar, almonds and salt in medium bowl; mix well. Add coconut oil; mix with fingertips until butter is evenly distributed and mixture is clumpy. Sprinkle evenly over fruit mixture. Place baking dish on prepared baking sheet.
5. Bake 50 minutes or until filling is bubbly and topping is golden brown. Cool 1 hour before serving.

ZUCCHINI BREAD

MAKES 1 LOAF (10 TO 12 SERVINGS)

- 2 cups all-purpose flour
- 1 teaspoon salt
- 1 teaspoon ground cinnamon
- ¾ teaspoon baking powder
- ¾ teaspoon baking soda
- ¼ teaspoon ground nutmeg
- ½ cup vegetable oil
- 2 eggs
- ½ cup granulated sugar
- ½ cup packed brown sugar
- 1 teaspoon vanilla
- 2 cups packed grated zucchini (2 to 3 medium)

1. Preheat oven to 350°F. Spray 9×5-inch loaf pan with nonstick cooking spray or line with parchment paper.
2. Combine flour, salt, cinnamon, baking powder, baking soda and nutmeg in medium bowl; mix well. Beat oil, eggs, granulated sugar, brown sugar and vanilla in large bowl until well blended. Add flour mixture; stir just until dry ingredients are moistened. Stir in zucchini until blended. Pour batter into prepared pan.
3. Bake 55 to 60 minutes or until toothpick inserted into center comes out clean. Cool in pan 20 minutes; remove to wire rack to cool completely.

CHAI SPICED BROWN RICE & CHIA PUDDING

MAKES 4 SERVINGS

- **4 English breakfast tea bags**
- **4 cups plain unsweetened soymilk or almond milk**
- **½ cup uncooked short grain brown rice, rinsed well**
- **¼ cup chia seeds**
- **2 tablespoons packed brown sugar**
- **2 tablespoons agave nectar**
- **1 teaspoon ground cinnamon**
- **½ teaspoon ground ginger**
- **¼ teaspoon salt**
- **¼ teaspoon ground cardamom**
- **¼ cup raisins**
- **Vegan whipped topping (optional)**

1. Pour 1 cup boiling water over tea bags in liquid measuring cup. Steep 5 minutes; discard tea bags.
2. Combine tea, soymilk, rice, chia seeds, brown sugar, agave, cinnamon, ginger, salt and cardamom in large saucepan. Bring to a boil over medium-high heat. Reduce heat to low.
3. Cook, partially covered, 1½ hours or until rice is tender and mixture is thick and creamy, stirring occasionally. Skim off any film that appears on surface. Stir in raisins.
4. Serve warm or at room temperature. Top with whipped topping, if desired.

FROSTED SPICE SWEET POTATO CAKE

MAKES 24 SERVINGS

- 6 tablespoons water
- 2 tablespoons ground flaxseed
- 1½ cups all-purpose flour
- 1¼ cups granulated sugar
- 2 teaspoons baking powder
- 1 teaspoon ground cinnamon
- ½ teaspoon baking soda
- ½ teaspoon salt
- ¼ teaspoon ground allspice
- 1 can (29 ounces) sweet potatoes, drained and mashed
- ¾ cup canola oil
- ½ cup chopped walnuts or pecans, plus additional for garnish
- ½ cup raisins
- No-Butter Buttercream Frosting (recipe follows)

1. Preheat oven to 325°F. Spray 13×9-inch baking pan with nonstick cooking spray. Combine water and flaxseed in small saucepan; simmer over medium-low heat 5 minutes. Cool to room temperature.
2. Combine flour, granulated sugar, baking powder, cinnamon, baking soda, salt and allspice in medium bowl. Beat mashed sweet potatoes, oil and flaxseed mixture in large bowl with electric mixer at low speed until blended. Add flour mixture; beat at medium speed 30 seconds or until well blended, scraping down bowl occasionally. Stir in ½ cup walnuts and raisins. Spoon batter into prepared pan.
3. Bake 35 to 40 minutes or until toothpick inserted into center comes out clean. Cool completely in pan on wire rack.
4. Prepare No-Butter Buttercream Frosting. Spread frosting over cake; sprinkle with additional walnuts. Store cake, covered, in refrigerator.

NO-BUTTER BUTTERCREAM FROSTING

MAKES ABOUT 4 CUPS

- ½ cup (1 stick) dairy-free margarine
- 2 teaspoons vanilla
- 4 cups powdered sugar
- 4 to 6 tablespoons soy creamer

1. Beat margarine in large bowl with electric mixer at medium speed until light and fluffy. Beat in vanilla.
2. Gradually beat in powdered sugar. Beat in soy creamer, 1 tablespoon at a time, until spreadable.

ORANGE NO-BUTTER BUTTERCREAM FROSTING

Reduce vanilla to 1 teaspoon and add the juice of half of an orange. Adjust texture with additional powdered sugar or soy creamer as needed.

CHOCOLATE NO-BUTTER BUTTERCREAM FROSTING

Replace ½ cup of the powdered sugar with ½ cup of unsweetened cocoa powder.

BLUEBERRY BANANA OATMEAL SMOOTHIE >

MAKES 2 SERVINGS

- 1 cup oatmilk
- 1 small ripe banana
- ½ cup frozen blueberries
- 1 container (5 ounces) nondairy yogurt (about ½ cup)
- ¼ cup quick oats

1. Combine oatmilk, banana and blueberries in blender; blend until smooth. Add yogurt and oats; blend until smooth.
2. Pour into two glasses.

SWEET BEET TREAT

MAKES 2 SERVINGS

- ¼ cup water
- 2 medium carrots, cut into chunks (about 4 ounces)
- 1 medium beet, peeled and cut into chunks
- 1 large sweet red apple, seeded and cut into chunks
- ¼ cup ice
- 1 tablespoon lemon juice
- 1 tablespoon maple syrup

Combine water, carrots, beet, apple, ice, lemon juice and maple syrup in blender; blend until smooth. Serve immediately.

OAT-APRICOT SNACK CAKE

MAKES 24 SERVINGS

- 1½ cups all-purpose flour
- 1 teaspoon baking soda
- 1 teaspoon ground cinnamon
- ½ teaspoon salt
- 1 container (6 ounces) plain soy yogurt
- ¾ cup packed brown sugar
- ½ cup granulated sugar
- ⅓ cup vegetable oil
- ¼ cup silken tofu, stirred until smooth
- 4 tablespoons orange juice, divided
- 2 teaspoons vanilla
- 2 cups old-fashioned oats
- 1 cup chopped dried apricots
- 1 cup powdered sugar

1. Preheat oven to 350°F. Spray 13×9-inch baking pan with nonstick cooking spray.
2. Combine flour, baking soda, cinnamon and salt in medium bowl. Whisk yogurt, brown sugar, granulated sugar, oil, tofu, 2 tablespoons orange juice and vanilla in large bowl. Add flour mixture; stir until blended. Stir in oats and apricots. Spread batter in prepared pan.
3. Bake 20 to 25 minutes or until toothpick inserted into center comes out clean. Cool completely in pan on wire rack.
4. Whisk powdered sugar and remaining 2 tablespoons orange juice in small bowl until smooth. Drizzle glaze over cake.

CARROT-SPICE SNACK CAKE

MAKES 8 SERVINGS

- ½ cup packed brown sugar
- ⅓ cup dairy-free margarine
- 2 eggs
- ½ cup soymilk or other dairy-free milk
- 1 teaspoon vanilla
- 1¼ cups all-purpose flour
- ¾ cup finely shredded carrot
- 2 teaspoons baking powder
- 1½ teaspoons pumpkin pie spice
- ½ teaspoon xanthan gum
- ½ teaspoon salt
- ⅓ cup golden raisins
- Powdered sugar

1. Preheat oven to 350°F. Spray 8-inch square baking pan with nonstick cooking spray.
2. Beat brown sugar and margarine in medium bowl with electric mixer at medium speed until well blended. Beat in eggs, soymilk and vanilla.
3. Stir in flour, carrot, baking powder, pumpkin pie spice, xanthan gum and salt. Stir in raisins.
4. Spread batter in prepared pan. Bake 25 to 30 minutes or until toothpick inserted into center comes out clean. Cool completely in pan on wire rack. Just before serving, sprinkle with powdered sugar.

PEANUT BUTTER CUPCAKES

MAKES 24 CUPCAKES

- 6 tablespoons water
- 2 tablespoons ground flaxseed
- 1 cup creamy peanut butter, divided
- ¼ cup (½ stick) dairy-free margarine, softened
- 1 cup packed brown sugar
- 2 cups all-purpose flour
- 2 teaspoons baking powder
- ½ teaspoon baking soda
- ½ teaspoon salt
- 1 cup vanilla soymilk
- 1½ cups mini semisweet chocolate chips, divided, plus additional for garnish
- Peanut Buttery Frosting (recipe follows)

1. Preheat oven to 350°F. Line 24 standard (2½-inch) muffin cups with paper baking cups. Combine water and flaxseed in small saucepan; simmer over medium-low heat 5 minutes. Cool to room temperature.
2. Beat ½ cup peanut butter and margarine in large bowl with electric mixer at medium speed until blended. Add brown sugar; beat until well blended. Beat in flaxseed mixture.
3. Whisk flour, baking powder, baking soda and salt in small bowl. Add flour mixture alternately with soymilk to peanut butter mixture; beat at low speed until well blended. Stir in 1 cup chocolate chips. Spoon batter evenly into prepared muffin cups.
4. Bake 15 minutes or until toothpick inserted into centers comes out clean. (Cover with foil if tops of cupcakes begin to brown too much.) Cool completely in pans on wire racks. Meanwhile, prepare Peanut Buttery Frosting.
5. Pipe or spread cupcakes with Peanut Buttery Frosting. Place remaining ½ cup peanut butter in small microwavable bowl. Microwave on HIGH 15 seconds or until melted. Place remaining ½ cup chocolate chips in another small microwavable bowl. Microwave on HIGH 15 seconds or until melted. Drizzle peanut butter and chocolate over frosting. Garnish with additional chocolate chips.

PEANUT BUTTERY FROSTING

Beat ½ cup (1 stick) dairy-free margarine and ½ cup creamy peanut butter in medium bowl with electric mixer at medium speed until smooth. Gradually add 1½ cups sifted powdered sugar and 1 teaspoon vanilla until blended. Add 2 to 6 tablespoons vanilla soymilk, 1 tablespoon at a time, until smooth. Makes about 3 cups.

INDEX

METRIC CONVERSION CHART

VOLUME MEASUREMENTS (dry)

1/8 teaspoon = 0.5 mL
1/4 teaspoon = 1 mL
1/2 teaspoon = 2 mL
3/4 teaspoon = 4 mL
1 teaspoon = 5 mL
1 tablespoon = 15 mL
2 tablespoons = 30 mL
1/4 cup = 60 mL
1/3 cup = 75 mL
1/2 cup = 125 mL
2/3 cup = 150 mL
3/4 cup = 175 mL
1 cup = 250 mL
2 cups = 1 pint = 500 mL
3 cups = 750 mL
4 cups = 1 quart = 1 L

VOLUME MEASUREMENTS (fluid)

1 fluid ounce (2 tablespoons) = 30 mL
4 fluid ounces (1/2 cup) = 125 mL
8 fluid ounces (1 cup) = 250 mL
12 fluid ounces (1 1/2 cups) = 375 mL
16 fluid ounces (2 cups) = 500 mL

WEIGHTS (mass)

1/2 ounce = 15 g
1 ounce = 30 g
3 ounces = 90 g
4 ounces = 120 g
8 ounces = 225 g
10 ounces = 285 g
12 ounces = 360 g
16 ounces = 1 pound = 450 g

DIMENSIONS

1/16 inch = 2 mm
1/8 inch = 3 mm
1/4 inch = 6 mm
1/2 inch = 1.5 cm
3/4 inch = 2 cm
1 inch = 2.5 cm

OVEN TEMPERATURES

250°F = 120°C
275°F = 140°C
300°F = 150°C
325°F = 160°C
350°F = 180°C
375°F = 190°C
400°F = 200°C
425°F = 220°C
450°F = 230°C

BAKING PAN SIZES

Utensil	Size in Inches/Quarts	Metric Volume	Size in Centimeters
Baking or Cake Pan (square or rectangular)	8×8×2	2 L	20×20×5
	9×9×2	2.5 L	23×23×5
	12×8×2	3 L	30×20×5
	13×9×2	3.5 L	33×23×5
Loaf Pan	8×4×3	1.5 L	20×10×7
	9×5×3	2 L	23×13×7
Round Layer Cake Pan	8×1½	1.2 L	20×4
	9×1½	1.5 L	23×4
Pie Plate	8×1¼	750 mL	20×3
	9×1¼	1 L	23×3
Baking Dish or Casserole	1 quart	1 L	—
	1½ quart	1.5 L	—
	2 quart	2 L	—